# Skunk Scout

# Skunk Scout

LAURENCE YEP

Houghton Mifflin Harcourt Edition

Printed in the United States of America

ISBN-13: 978-0-547-07397-2
ISBN-10: 0-547-07397-6


10 1083   15 14 13
4500422765

## Also by Laurence Yep

AMERICAN DRAGONS:
Twenty-five Asian American Voices

CHILD OF THE OWL

COCKROACH COOTIES

DRAGON OF THE LOST SEA

DRAGON WAR

DRAGON'S GATE

DRAGONWINGS

HIROSHIMA

THE JOURNAL OF WONG MING-CHUNG
A Chinese Miner

LADY OF CH'IAO KUO
Warrior of the South

LATER, GATOR

THE LOST GARDEN

RAINBOW PEOPLE

THE SERPENT'S CHILDREN

THE STAR FISHER

To my **U**ncle **F**rancis,
camper and abalone diver

# Skunk Scout

# ONE ⋀

**For the first nine years of my life,** I had a deal with Mother Nature: I stayed on asphalt in the city where I belonged, and she stayed on dirt in the country.

Why would anyone leave Chinatown? It had everything a kid could want: comic books, cheap snacks, and kung fu movies.

If I wanted to see wildlife, I could watch the rats play around the restaurant trash cans. And I could always get another pet cockroach like Hercules.

Then I turned the big one-o. And Mother Nature stomped all over me as if I were cheap cardboard.

My birthday started out just fine. There was a big sheet cake from Ping Yuen and lichee ice cream

1

from Fong and Fong's. There were also plenty of presents. Almost all of them were toys and books, too. Grandmother gave me a football—though she told me I probably didn't deserve it.

Even Cousin Alice gave me a real gift. She worked in her family's store on Grant Avenue, where all the tourists go in Chinatown. Though the store was supposed to sell Chinese art goods, it sold mostly novelty items. Like her father, my uncle Mat, Alice was a big practical joker. One year she gave me a telescope that left a black ring around my eye, and last year it had been a baseball glove filled with itching powder.

This time, though, her present was something useful—a hand buzzer.

"What's it for?" my little brother, Bobby, asked.

"You'll find out." I grinned.

"Not if you want to sit down the rest of the week," Father warned me. But that was okay. I'm not one of those people who need to have their fun right away. I could use it on Bobby in a week or two when my parents weren't around.

Aunt Norma gave me her usual practical gift: underwear. This year, though, I had even that covered. My classmate Lincoln's parents owned a clothing store on Grant Avenue. I could slip Lincoln any clothes—as long as they were in the original package—and get thirty cents on the dollar.

My little brother, Bobby, gave me a handmade book. Each page was good for one hug. That was just like Bobby, too. Of course, everyone said, "Aaaaw . . ."

There was a time when I couldn't stand my little brother. Bobby had grown on me, though. How could you dislike someone who kept forgiving you? And Bobby had even saved me from a bully named Arnie-zilla. (Okay, so what if I do get him with the buzzer? I used to do a lot worse things to him. I had to stay in practice, after all.)

I put a smile on my face and told him I liked his present.

"Really?" he asked, excited. Jumping to his feet, he waded through the wrapping paper. "Then you can have a hug for free right now."

When Bobby had plopped back down, I picked up the gift from Uncle Curtis, Aunt Ethel, and Cousin Nancy. That was the real joker in the deck.

Their presents were always a combination of

Aunt Norma's and Cousin Alice's. Like Aunt Norma, they gave you what they thought you needed, not what you wanted. And like Cousin Alice's, their gifts had sometimes been useful for teasing Bobby.

One year they had given me a bird-watching guide. It came in real handy in Chinatown, where there are only pigeons—which come in two types: dirty and dirtier.

Last year, I'd gotten a box of healthy candy made out of broccoli. For once, I'd had some fun with one of their presents. I slipped the hard, sticky lumps in Bobby's bed and shoes. Then I watched him squirm. Not only were the candies as hard as rocks, but they stuck to you, too. The manufacturer should have been selling them in novelty shops rather than in health food stores.

My family calls me the boy with X-ray eyes, but I'm just good at guessing what's inside a gift box. This one, though, didn't rattle when I shook it. And it was light—too light to be a book or candy.

Stumped, I tore off the Christmas paper. (No one bothers with good paper for me, because I'm a ripper.)

Inside the box was a pile of tissue paper. I dug around until I found the bottle of mosquito repellent. "Ha, ha, ha. Very funny," I said with a grin. Then I started digging around in the paper underneath it.

Uncle Curtis cleared his throat. "Don't bother looking anymore, Teddy. That's it."

"Oh, well, thanks a lot," I said, wondering if Lincoln's parents sold mosquito repellent, too.

Uncle Curtis suddenly sprang to his feet and tried to imitate a game show host. "B-u-u-t that's not all. You also have a deluxe ticket on the Fun Express with me!"

Fun was one word I never would have associated with Uncle Curtis. He was such a stuffed shirt. He liked to find any excuse to frown. "Where's it going?" I asked.

Uncle Curtis spread his arms. "The Fun Express will whisk you away for three days and two fun-filled nights of camping on Mount Tamalpais! I'm even going to take a personal day to do that."

"Camping?" I asked, shocked.

"A-a-a-nd—" Uncle Curtis said, raising his index finger, "you get to take along a guest of your choice—provided it's Bobby."

Bobby started hopping up and down. "Neat-o," he kept repeating over and over.

The last thing I wanted on earth was to be stuck in the wilderness with Uncle Curtis. So I looked to my parents for help.

But Father smiled reassuringly. "We already gave Curtis our okay."

"Are you going, too?" Bobby asked Cousin Nancy.

Aunt Ethel shook her head violently. "Nancy and I went camping."

"Just once," Uncle Curtis said.

"Once was enough," Cousin Nancy said.

Fortunately, Grandmother rode to my rescue. "No," she said. Though she was a tiny woman, she had a megaphone voice. She'd gotten good lungs from years of shouting over the clacking of mah-jong tiles. "You get lost going to the bathroom, Curtis."

Uncle Curtis rubbed the back of his head. "I know the route, Mama."

Aunt Ethel nodded. "He's got a map. And I marked the way."

"But can he read it?" Uncle Mat wondered.

Grandmother stuck out her chin defiantly. "Well, you aren't taking Teddy and Bobby anywhere. They'll get eaten by bears." She liked keeping her family where she could watch over them.

I was pleased, in a way. Grandmother was usually scolding me, but I guess deep down inside she really cared.

"No bear would eat Teddy, Mama. They'd get indigestion for sure," Uncle Mat teased.

Grandmother shrugged. "Curtis is too big, so I can't stop him if he wants to get eaten. But I won't let him take the boys."

"But I've got it all planned, Mama," Uncle Curtis complained.

"Curtis," Aunt Ethel said, "if it's going to make your mother unhappy, maybe you should forget about it."

"But, Mama," Uncle Curtis coaxed, "they've got to learn there's more to life than Chinatown."

"That's what television is for," Grandmother said stubbornly. Those were my sentiments exactly.

Uncle Mat stuffed his hands into his pockets. "It's not like when we were kids. No one's going to hurt them just because they're outside of Chinatown."

"The times have changed." Aunt Norma nodded. "Today it's safe for us Chinese to go most anywhere."

Grandmother considered that for a moment and then shook her head. "Maybe the rules for people have changed, but bears are bears."

The camping trip would have died right there if it hadn't been for Bobby.

"It would be neat-o to see all sorts of animals," Bobby begged Grandmother.

My little brother has this trick. He can make his eyes as big as saucers—almost as big as Bambi's.

It almost worked on Grandmother, but not quite. "And what happens when the animals see you?"

Bobby got this funny look on his face. "Then the animals better watch out because I'm plenty strong." He pretended to make a muscle.

Grandmother gave a snort. "What could a little thing like you do?"

"I'm even stronger than my uncles," Bobby insisted.

Grandmother immediately blamed me. "You've been teaching Bobby how to fib."

I held up my arms. "I'm innocent," I protested. Bobby couldn't have told a lie if his life depended on it.

Bobby leaned against Grandmother's chair. "If I show you, Grandmother," he wheedled, "may Teddy and I go?"

Grandmother folded her arms skeptically. "All right."

So Bobby went to a shelf and got two books. He set them down on the table. Opening them, he shoved them toward one another. Painstakingly, he mixed the pages together almost one by one. When he was done, the books looked like they were fused together.

Then he stepped back. "I bet you can't pull the books apart, Uncle Curtis."

Uncle Curtis just gave a laugh. "Don't be silly, Bobby." He grabbed a book spine in either hand and tugged. The books, though, were stuck together as if they were glued. So he yanked harder. Still they stay fused. Uncle Curtis tried harder. His face turned bright red and he made funny noises. A vein on his forehead popped out in a green knot.

Finally he put them down. "I give up," he panted.

"You've got no muscles, Curtis. Let a real man do it." Uncle Mat grinned. Picking up the books confidently, he began to pull. His smile changed to a frown.

"Where're your big muscles now, Mat?" Uncle Curtis teased.

"I'll get it," Uncle Mat grunted. He strained at the books so hard he spun around in a circle. In the end, he dumped them down on the table. "Stupid books," he said angrily. "You try it, Harold."

Father, though, shook his head. "I've lived with Bobby long enough to know better. If he says we can't do it, then we can't."

"Anyone else want to try?" Bobby asked the room.

The rest of us agreed with Father, so we refused.

Bobby stepped up to the books and opened them, flipping the pages so they separated again. When there were only a few pages left, he pulled the books apart easily.

"But why did the books stick together?" Uncle Curtis asked, puzzled.

"I read it in a book," Bobby said. "All paper is made from fiber, and the fibers stick together. It doesn't matter how smooth the paper feels to our hands."

"You're not going to get a bear to fall for that trick," Grandmother said.

"But that's the point," Bobby said. "It's brain, not brawn, that counts."

Grandmother was beginning to relent. "And feet, too," she reminded him.

"I'm good at running," Bobby said with a glance at me. He had to be fast to get away from me.

Grandmother was sharp enough to understand. "Yes, I bet Teddy's trained you good."

"That's what big brothers are for," I mumbled.

"We'll be real careful," Bobby promised.

Grandmother voiced her other big fear. "But the ground will be cold and damp, and children's chests are so weak. You'll get pneumonia for sure." Grandmother herself was armored in layers of clothing against the chill. She wore a blouse, vest, and sweater—even in eighty-degree weather.

"We'll have ground cloths and sleeping bags and tents," Uncle Curtis assured her.

She bit her lip thoughtfully. "Well, maybe this camping wouldn't be such a bad thing after all."

"Neat-o," Bobby squealed. "May I practice with a sleeping bag?"

Uncle Curtis grinned. Bobby's reaction was probably what he'd expected from me. "You may come over to our place and borrow some camping gear anytime."

Bobby turned around happily to say something to me but stopped when he saw my face. "But if you'd rather go with just Uncle Curtis, that's okay." He'd misunderstood my disgusted expression.

He'd made it obvious how much he wanted to go. For a moment, I thought about being mean and making him stay home.

I could feel everyone's eyes on me. I knew they didn't want me to disappoint Bobby. Besides, did I really want to be alone with Uncle Curtis?

"You can come," I said through gritted teeth.

I just shut my eyes. This had to be God's punishment for all the tricks I'd ever pulled on my little brother.

#

The next morning when I woke up, Bobby had already left the room. So I just lay there, enjoying the silence. No facts about cockroaches. No details about alligators. Just blessed quiet.

Then Father knocked at the door. "Time to get up. You're helping out at the store."

I pulled the covers over my head. "Five more minutes."

Father rapped on the door again. "Come on, sleepyhead. Bobby's already been to Curtis's to borrow the camping gear."

I got out of bed reluctantly. I was going to leave it the way it was. However, as always, Bobby had made up his. So I wound up making my own, after all.

13

When I finished washing up, he was already on his stomach in front of the television.

As the roars thundered from the television, I grinned. Great! There was nothing like early-morning mayhem. "Which episode of *Wolf Warriors* is this?"

Bobby held a finger to his lips. "Shh."

The bear had real fur though. "Hey, that's no cartoon."

"It's a nature show, *Wilderness Scout*," Bobby said, without turning around.

"We always watch *Wolf Warriors* at this time," I complained and started to reach for the dial.

"But we've seen every *Wolf Warriors* a hundred times," Bobby protested. "I'm studying for the trip." Then he hesitated. "I'm sorry, Teddy. I'm being selfish." He started to reach for the television to change it to my cartoon.

"Teddy!" Mother called from the kitchen. She had ears as sensitive as a bat's—at least when I was doing something wrong.

"But this is on polar bears," I called back.

"Well, it's on bears, but I could change it if you want," Bobby offered.

"If there really are going to be any kind of bears, we shouldn't go," I said in a loud voice to make sure Mother would hear.

"You know Bobby. He loves anything with nature," Mother said. "Leave the television set alone."

"Okay, but it's my turn tomorrow," I grumbled. I went into the kitchen to get my official *Wolf Warriors* cereal.

"Not that," Mother said as I started to reach into the cabinet. "Bobby already got your breakfast ready."

"Oh . . . that was nice of him," I said, wondering if I should test for poison. But I found it was worse.

When I looked inside the bowl, I didn't recognize a thing in there. "What's this stuff?"

Mother held up a box with a grinning tree full of spotted owls. "It's some kind of campers' breakfast mix." She read the label. " 'Certified to give you the boost you need for camping and hiking.' "

I poked around at the contents. Was this some kind of practical joke? But Bobby had no sense of humor. "It looks like tanbark from the playground."

"Bobby brought it back when he went to borrow some camping gear from Uncle Curtis. He wants to practice eating outdoor kind of meals," Mother said.

I picked up a piece and showed it to Mother. "This looks like a twig."

"Don't be silly," Mother said. She made a face when she took it and ate it but managed to choke out, "See, it's fine."

Bobby must have overheard us, because he came to the doorway right then during a commercial break. "You don't have to eat it, Teddy. I just thought you might like to try it."

Mother frowned. I knew she didn't want to disappoint my little brother. "No, I want to," I sighed.

As I crunched my way through my official camper's breakfast, I could smell the bacon and eggs cooking on the stove and the bread toasting.

While Mother and Father ate, I tried to distract myself with some television. But the bears were eating a seal. From the way they chowed down, I would have been willing to try blubber.

I could still smell the bacon on Father's breath as we left home.

We lived on Clay Street above Powell, so it was a steep walk down to the fish store. Between the tall buildings, I could see a blue square that was the bay. Oakland was a smudge hidden in the haze on the horizon. Somewhere in the distance, I heard the clang of a cable car bell.

The coffee shops and bakeries had opened long ago. The smell of tea and coffee mixed with the smell of fresh bread and cakes.

The Chinese crullers smelled especially delicious after a breakfast of twigs and bark and pebbles. The crullers aren't sweet at all, but they taste of the oil in which they are fried. They're supposed to be eaten with rice porridge.

Mr. Soo was setting up a board on milk crates outside his store. On the shelf, he would put bins of vegetables. He called out a hello to us. And the little old ladies were already elbowing one another at Orange Land to get the best fruit. Football linemen could have learned a few tricks from them.

Big trucks rumbled up and down the narrow streets to make deliveries. Sometimes they barely squeezed between the parked cars.

The restaurants had their back doors open.

Through the doorways floated the sound of Chinese music and loud voices as the cooks cut up meat and vegetables for the lunch crowd.

Women gossiped about last night's Chinese televison soap opera as they headed into the alleys where the sweatshops were located. There they would sew clothes for some of the fanciest shops in San Francisco.

Yawning people plodded past us, headed for bed. These were men and women who might be janitors in the tall office buildings that surround Chinatown. Or they might be bellboys or workers from the night shift in the ritzy hotels above us on Nob Hill.

This was Chinatown. This was my home. It fit me as snug as a glove.

We turned up an alley, and Father unlocked the back door to our fish store. Then we stepped into the cool, pungent shadows. I know it sounds odd, but I liked this moment the best, before Father turned on the light. At this moment I could pretend I was inside the under-sea cavern of the Dragon King. The distant black bulk was his throne. The tall shapes, his guards.

The dim outline of a door, his treasure vault.

Once Father flipped the switch, everything became ordinary. The bulky object was the counter. The tall shapes were aprons hanging from hooks. The door was labeled FREEZER.

Father and I had just put on big rubber boots when Bobby asked permission to go to the library. "I want to do research for the camping trip," he explained. "I'll be back in thirty minutes."

But the half hour swelled into an hour and then another. Finally I couldn't take it anymore. After hosing off the sidewalk outside, I clopped back into the store in my rubber boots.

The concrete floor behind the counter could get wet and slippery, so Father had put down long two-by-fours. I walked along the worn boards. "Bobby's been away a long time."

Father just shrugged. "You know Bobby. You put him in a room of books, and he's lost for the day."

"Well," I said, "maybe I ought to go to the library, too."

Father squatted down by a crate. "Do you even know where it is?" he teased.

"I'll follow the groove Bobby's worn into the sidewalk," I said.

As he opened the lid, he grunted, "No."

"How come you let Bobby go and not me?" I asked.

He lifted out a halibut. "If I thought you'd really use the library, I'd let you go. But you'll just goof off."

"How do you know that?" I asked guiltily. That was exactly what I had been planning to do.

Father slapped the halibut down onto a black plastic tray filled with ice. "Because I was exactly like you when I was your age."

"You were?" I said in surprise.

"When Bobby grows up, he'll be a doctor or scientist," Father predicted.

"Well, what if I want to be a scientist, too?" I said.

A corner of Father's mouth curled up. "Who wanted to watch cartoons this morning and who wanted to watch the nature show?"

"That was just this morning," I said.

"And you're like that every morning. And after-noon. And nighttime, too," Father picked up a clam from another tray. "You're just like this fellow. He's happy inside his little shell, doing the same things every day."

I tried to remember an example to prove Father was wrong, but I guess I was in a rut. I swallowed. "And what do you think I'll be?"

"You'll get the store," he said.

"Unh . . . thank you," I said. That seemed to be the polite thing to say.

Father fiddled with the chips of ice in the tray. "There's no shame in owning a fish store, Teddy." I could hear the hurt in his voice.

I didn't know what to say. It was hard to argue without insulting him. "I didn't say there was."

"It's a smelly business, but it pays our bills," he said defensively.

I didn't know why Father was pointing out the obvious to me. "And we're grateful."

He dumped the clam back on top of its family. The shell made a loud clacking sound. "I know. But fish-store owners don't get their names in the newspapers. And no one grows up saying that they want to own a fish store. I certainly didn't when I was your age." He began to put out the rest of the halibut. "But you'll pay your bills, too."

While Bobby became the famous scientist, I thought.

I just stood there for a moment. Part of me wanted to make up with Father. But part of me resented what he was doing to me.

When I couldn't think of what to say, I retreated to the storeroom. I should have been tearing up the old crates. However, I just sat down. For some reason, I felt like crying. I told myself it was stupid. Father had just said I was going to get the business.

That meant he really did care about me.

And yet I felt just like one of his fish. Halibut goes into the halibut tray. Snapper goes into the snapper tray. Bobby gets to go into the scientist tray. But Teddy stays on the fish-store tray. I was only ten, but Father had my whole life planned.

I don't know how long Father was in the doorway watching me. I just know he was there when I finally looked up.

He held out some money. "Hey, let's get something special for lunch. Why don't you go to Sam Wo and get us some *gwoon fun*?"

Gwoon fun are sheets of rice noodles that are rolled up into cylinders with barbecued pork and other tasty things. Then they are sliced up into bite-size pieces.

I knew he was trying to make up with me in his own way. "I feel more like chicken buns," I said.

He waved the dollar bills at me. "No. Get the gwoon fun."

And then it hit me: gwoon fun was Bobby's favorite, not mine.

It figured.

Who was this camping trip really for? Me or Bobby?

As I washed my hands, I pretended my favorite game: I was an only child. No more torn comic books. No more lost toys. And the closet and the shelves would be mine, all mine!

And best of all, no twerp to make me go camping!

# ⓉⒽⓇⒺⒺ

**I got the gwoon fun,** but I didn't eat much of it. So there was a lot left for Bobby when he came back. At first, all I saw was a huge stack of books coming through the doorway. Then I realized it had shoes like Bobby's.

Father grinned from ear to ear as he turned to me. "Do you see the walking library, Teddy?"

"Yeah, it's a lot of books," I said. The little showoff!

Bobby peeked around the stack. "Is it lunch time already? I lost track of the time."

"We figured," Father said, pretending to be gruff.

"I'm sorry," Bobby said to Father and then to

me. He really meant it, too. My little brother might be a pest, but he was no goof-off—not like me.

"Well, you can make up for it after you've had lunch," Father said and took the books from Bobby.

When Bobby looked inside the carton, his eyes lit up. "Neat-o," he said. "Aren't you going to eat any, too?" he asked.

"We already finished," Father said, setting the books down on a chair.

Bobby glanced at me and then grinned at Father. "Maybe tomorrow we can have some *guy bow*." Guy bow are chicken-filled buns, and my favorite. It was just like my little brother to think about me.

"In every book I read, the animals ate and ate. They made me so hungry," Bobby explained, as he began to wolf the white cylinders down. Bobby might be smart; but when it came to gwoon fun, he had the table manners of a pig.

"I guess I'd feel starved, too," Father said and winked at me. "Wouldn't you, Teddy?"

I thought about all the time I'd spent working

with smelly fish while Bobby had just sat in the library. "I wouldn't know about books." I shrugged. "I only get excited by fish." At least that's what Father seemed to think.

Surprised, Father stared at me as if he were trying to figure out what to say. But he wasn't having any more luck than I was. So he picked up one of Bobby's books. "What you'd check out?" he asked.

"I found stuff on the wildlife of the Bay Area," Bobby bubbled. "I bet we'll run into some of them on Mount Tamalpais."

"Yeah? Like what?" Father sat down on a stool and sighed. "Boy, that feels good, to rest my dogs for a while."

"Your bunions hurting you?" Bobby asked sympathetically.

They were always bothering him, but Father wasn't the kind to complain. "They'll be okay in a little bit." He began thumbing through the book, looking for pictures. It was the same thing I would have done when I first handled a book.

I just left. He was busy listening to Bobby. I knew I wouldn't be missed. After all, there were all those bins that needed to be washed and cleaned. And if the store was going to be mine, I ought to be the one to do it.

I know Father thought he was doing his best for me. I tried to tell myself it was okay. After all, a clam was a clam, and it was stuck on the beach. Still, there must be some clam somewhere that must want to swim free in the ocean. Well, the clam was stupid too. It couldn't change what it was. And neither could I.

Later, Bobby did try to apologize to me for staying away so long. "I'm sorry, Teddy. I didn't mean to stick you with all the chores." He scratched his cheek sheepishly. "You know I lose track of time when I'm in a library."

I knew all too well. "Forget it," I shrugged.

"I'll make it up to you," he promised.

I will give Bobby this. The rest of the day my little brother worked twice as hard as I did—even though he was dying to sit down and read his books.

If I had spare time, I'd be down at the playground with my friends. Or watching television. Or munching popcorn in a movie theater. So maybe it wasn't so bad to be a clam. But then Mrs. Wong came in. She was our landlady, and nothing was ever fresh enough for her.

She was walking down the aisle between two long tables. Every now and then she'd stop and bend over and sniff. So far nothing had passed the nose test.

I was adding some sand dabs to a tray on one of the tables as she passed. "Everything is so old. Especially these crabs!"

"I'm sorry you think so, ma'am. We just got them in yesterday," I said politely.

She pointed at her nose. "Don't try to fool me. This nose knows."

I forced myself to be patient, just as Father would. "Yes, ma'am."

Having put me in my place, she waddled on, and I turned back to my sand dabs.

"Ai-i-ee!" she shouted suddenly.

I'd never heard her get that excited before. Maybe she'd finally found something fresh enough for her.

When I turned, she was rubbing her behind. "How dare you!" she glared.

"Ma'am?" I asked, puzzled.

"You pinched me," she accused.

I held up a sand dab in either hand. "My hands were full."

"Well, someone did," she said.

I flapped a sand dab toward a tray next to her. A crab peered over the edge, bubbles coming from its mouth. "I bet it was a crab."

"Why would it do that?" she demanded.

"Because it's so fresh?" I suggested hopefully.

Well, that really set off Mrs. Wong. Father hurried over to calm her down. I just stood there, blinking as she jabbed an angry finger at me. Did I really want a lifetime of this?

She wound up leaving with the crab and a free pound of scallops.

When she was gone, Father sighed to me, "Teddy, it doesn't matter if the customer is unpleasant. You've got to learn to keep your mouth shut."

"Yes, sir," I said. However, I was beginning to see the drawbacks to a clam's life.

At about five o'clock, Father told us to go home.

Mother worked part-time for Uncle Mat. The summer brought loads of tourists into Chinatown, so they did a landslide in business. A chunk of it was souvenirs, of course, but they made a lot of money on sweatshirts, too. Because San Francisco is in California, tourists assume San Francisco will be hot. But it isn't. One of our chores was to cook the rice, chop up the vegetables, and slice the meat or fish. Mother or Father would make it later—whoever got home first.

"Let me make it up to you for this morning," Bobby said. "You just leave all the chores to me."

See what I mean? It was hard to dislike Bobby for long.

He even let me wash up first. I scrubbed my hands with soap good and hard. Then, curious, I sniffed my hands. There was still a faint smell of fish on my palms. I tried to clean off the scent a half dozen times. No matter how hard I tried, it clung to my skin.

I had never noticed it before. Maybe it was because Father always smelled like our store. I suppose I would, too.

When I came out, Bobby had already washed up at the kitchen sink. He was washing the rice now. At the same time, he had a book propped open so he could read. That was so typical.

I drifted over to the television set and snapped it on. It had been left on the educational channel from that morning. There was another nature documentary on now. I wondered if they ever ran out of animals for these shows.

This one was on snakes, which I don't like. I was going to snap it over to a cartoon, but I stopped. Maybe a clam had to stay a clam. But a human was different. We could be anything we wanted. And maybe I wouldn't have to put up with Mrs. Wong all my life.

So I left it on. I'd show Father that he was wrong.

However, I can't say I remember much. The only part I liked was when a snake ate a frog. I didn't know they could open their jaws that wide.

I was still watching it when Bobby called from the kitchen. "Aren't the cartoons on?"

I shrugged. "I thought I'd watch this."

"You don't have to do that for my sake," he said, looking guilty.

"Maybe *I* want to watch it," I snapped.

"Okay, okay," he said. He passed through the living room into the dining room and began to set the table.

"Do they have snakes up on Mount Tamalpais?" I called to him.

"Lots of them," he said.

"But they're all harmless, right?" I asked.

"No, they have rattlesnakes," he said, coming back in.

Suddenly I realized the nature show was a matter of life or death. "But not where we're camping, right?"

"I don't know, but rattlesnakes are probably all over. They've been there a lot longer than humans," Bobby said. I heard him open a door.

There was a series of thumps. I turned around to see that Bobby had tried to open the closet door. He forgot to ease it open, though. The closet was so jammed that an avalanche of stuff tumbled down. I turned around to see if I was going to have to dig out my brother. The clothes and boxes had knocked him onto his seat, but he was still alive.

"What are you doing?" I asked.

"I thought I'd practice with the camping gear," Bobby said, pulling himself out of the landslide. "Look at all the neat stuff Uncle Curtis loaned us."

It was hidden on the bottom of the pile, so we had to dig it out first. Bobby tried to stack the boxes and junk neatly in the closet. I just pitched it back in with both hands.

Uncle Curtis had army-surplus sleeping bags for both Bobby and me. There were also a couple of canteens, one from army surplus. The other was a Girl Scout canteen. It must have belonged to Cousin Nancy.

"This is what I wanted," Bobby said. He lifted out two metal boxes. They were flat on the top and bottom and oval in shape. "Look at this! Isn't it neat-o?" He undid some screws on one of them and slid a bar back. The container split into two parts that could be used as a plate and a bowl. Inside were small knives and forks.

"I want to get used to eating with these," he explained. "I only put out three places."

I was going to tell him that was dumb because

we had perfectly good plates. I stopped myself, though. It seemed like a real clammish thing to say. After all, clams always followed the same routine.

Instead, I took the other kit. "You can take away my setting. I'll use this one," I said.

Of course, that evening, Bobby didn't want to sleep in his bed. Instead, he spread a ground cloth on the floor. "The sleeping bag is what I really want to get used to."

"The floor's going to be hard," I said.

"It can't be any worse than the ground," Bobby said, unrolling his bag over the ground cloth.

I felt the mattress. It was soft and a lot more comfortable than down there. That seemed like another clammish attitude, though.

"Move over." I sighed. "I'm going to sleep in my bag, too."

"Isn't this fun?" Bobby said.

"Yeah, loads of laughs," I grumbled. It was going to be hard being a nonclam.

The sleeping bag didn't have much padding though, and the ground cloth had none. Bobby was snoring away in minutes. I tossed and turned, trying to find a comfortable position.

About midnight, I gave up and crawled back into bed. I was just like the clam. I felt like such a failure. Maybe Father was right.

I can't say I slept well, though. I kept dreaming I was a giant clam, and Mrs. Wong was trying to cook me.

# FOUR

**When I woke the next morning,** I just lay there for a long time. On the one hand, I liked Chinatown. On the other hand, I hated to be told it was the only place I could live. It would always be my home, but why couldn't I come back to it after a lot of adventures?

Bobby was willing to chase a butterfly around the world. I ought to be able to go more than six blocks.

I decided right then and there that I'd prove that Father was wrong about me. I was just as smart as Bobby, and an expert at one thing Bobby wasn't: I knew how to cheat.

Getting out of bed, I tiptoed over my sleeping

brother. His stack of books lay near the dresser. Squatting, I tried to read the spines. It was hard, though, with the blinds down. I had to lean closer and squint. All the titles sounded the same. I started to yawn just looking at them.

Then I heard Bobby begin to stir. Quickly, I grabbed the first book from on top and hid it beneath dirty clothes in the corner. As the final touch, I lay some of my dirty socks on top. I was sure Bobby would never go near the pile now.

I figured that was one book that I would read and he wouldn't. Then I'd have my own facts to impress people.

That morning we had Spam and eggs with toast. I only nibbled at the fatty slab. It was just too greasy and salty. After trying it, Bobby wasn't too crazy about Spam, either. "Maybe it will taste better when we're outdoors," he said hopefully.

"And starving," Father joked. Bobby ate his anyway, though. I just shoved my plate to the side.

Just as he had the day before, Bobby went over to the library. He said he wanted to look up something, but he lost track of time again.

I was feeling sorry for myself as I began to open the crates of fish.

"Not that one," Father said. He came rushing over. "Those lobster tails are in dry ice."

"What's dry ice?" I peeked into the crate and saw what looked like a slab of regular ice.

I started to reach in to touch it, but Father stopped me. "You could get your fingers stuck to it. It's much colder than normal ice. See? It's frozen solid as a rock." He rapped a knuckle on it. "You better let me handle these. Will you find the ice chest and wash it out? Curtis wants to use it when you go camping. We'll put ice in it the night before."

"Spam comes in a can, though," I said.

Father winked. "I think Curtis has plans for a better menu, but don't tell Bobby. He's having too much fun practicing."

I was glad we weren't going to have Spam, so I searched extra hard for the ice chest. It was an old aluminum one. When I lowered the handles, I also unlocked the lid. It was pretty dusty inside. As I began to clean it, though, I suddenly had an idea.

The problem with the regular ice was that it would melt fast even in the ice chest. It would only keep food cold for only so long. But what if we used dry ice? I bet it would keep everything cold for the whole trip.

Bobby wasn't the only smart one in the family.

Next day, the Spam tasted even worse. It was like eating a slab of salt mixed with grease. "I can't eat this," I said, shoving it away from me.

"There's always the cereal," Mother said.

Twigs and leaves were just as unappetizing. It was bad enough that I was going to sleep on the cold, hard ground. I wasn't going to be hungry, too. Food was more important than anything else. Despite Father's hints about our camp menu, I didn't trust Uncle Curtis.

So this time when we got to the store, I beat Bobby to the punch. "Can I go to the library?" I asked Father.

He was wrapping a fish in paper for a customer. "Are you really going to get a book, or are you going to see a movie at the Hub?"

"I'm not going there," I said indignantly.

He studied me for a while. Then he slid the

bundle into a bag. "I suppose you deserve some time off."

I felt guilty, because Father never got to take breaks even when his bunions hurt him. And if anyone deserved a rest, he did.

"Maybe you can pick up some guy bow for lunch, too," Bobby piped up. He hadn't forgotten.

Father gave me some money; but I didn't head for the library or the deli first. If I was going to survive this trip, I was going to need more than Spam.

I began to walk along confidently. This was my turf. If you wanted the best comics or best lunch or best toys in Chinatown, just come to me.

Feeling better, I aimed for my favorite stall. It was located against the outside wall of a store. Long shelves ran the length of the building, and there were doors that could be fitted over the shelves at night.

There were all sorts of cheap toys and souvenirs—pop guns and little wooden snakes that wriggled and plastic back scratchers and other stuff. There were a half dozen tourists snatching up those items to bring home. However, I went over to a section where none of them would go.

I studied the glass jars ranged along on the green shelf. The labels were in Chinese, so I could only read a few words. But I knew all the goodies by sight.

There were three different kinds of preserved plums—salty, medium, and sweet. Next to them were strips of sugar-coated coconut. I was a little uneasy about the way they curled like snakes. But I really went for the candied ginger. The narrow ribbons were a fiery orange-red, and just as hot to eat as to look at.

Bobby and Uncle Curtis could get ready in their way. I'd get ready in mine. I was going to load up on candy.

When the tourists were gone, the owner came over.

"I'll have a quarter pound of those," I said, pointing to the sweet plums.

"Ver-ee tas-tee." He nodded.

"And the same for those," I said, indicating the lemon strips.

"Ver-ee health-ee," he assured me.

41

"And four ounces of the coconut," I said.

"Ver-ee sweet-ee." He grinned.

"And the ginger," I said.

He puckered his mouth but nodded approvingly. "Ver-ee spi-cee."

He weighed everything and put it all into little paper sacks. Then, my pockets bulging, I hurried to the deli, where I got some guy bow for lunch. Then I went on to the library on Powell Street. Father had not said how long my break was supposed to be. I was sure, though, that I had used up most of it; and I knew I couldn't get away with Bobby's excuse that I'd gotten absorbed in my reading.

As always, the Chinatown branch was full of people. I just grabbed the first book I could and went to the checkout desk.

When I presented my library card, the librarian smiled. "Did you just move here?" she asked.

"No, I was born here," I said.

"Oh, it's just that your card looks so new," she said and then saw my name. "Are you any relation to Bobby?"

"He's my brother," I admitted.

"And our best customer," she said, stamping the book.

As I entered the fish store, I made a point of displaying the book in front of me.

Bobby had been refreshing the ice in the trays. He waddled over in his rubber boots when he saw me. "What did you take out?"

Leave it to him to ruin my alibi.

I slipped the book behind me. "Something really useful."

"I didn't think you were interested in reading anything," Father said from behind me. He snatched the book from me and squinted as he read the title on the spine. "*Sewing Made Easy?*"

I wished now that I had taken a few more minutes and found a proper book. "What if the tent gets a tear in it?"

Father chuckled. "Or maybe you have to stitch up the gashes a bear makes on your arm."

Bobby, though, took me seriously. "That's real good thinking, Teddy."

Relieved that he'd restored my alibi, I patted him on the back. "That's what older brothers are for."

The rest of the week I tried to practice camping with Bobby. The more I practiced, though, the less I liked it. I wanted to sleep in beds where there were no rattlesnakes. I wanted to eat beef rice plates. Above all, I wanted television.

I almost thought about chickening out, but it would have been even more shameful to stay behind. So instead, when I could, I'd sneak the wildlife book out and read it. But I might just as well have been reading the telephone book. It was chock-full of Latin names and botanical terms.

I tried to look at the pictures and memorize what I could of the text, but nothing would stay. As soon as I learned one plant, the next one would push it out of my brain.

Saturday morning came all too fast. I hardly slept the night before. I kept dreaming about bears. It seemed just as I had fallen asleep, Bobby was shaking my shoulder.

"Rise and shine, Mr. Camper," he whispered to me.

I opened my eyelids a crack. There was only

44

dim light in the room, because the sun had not risen yet.

My eyes only half open, I got ready. I thought condemned prisoners could get a hot meal at least. I only got more twigs and bark in milk.

Mother must have heard us because she shuffled into the kitchen. "Have you got everything?" She yawned.

All our gear lay piled by the door. "Yes," I said. My jaws stretched in a yawn, too. I guess it was catching.

My own emergency supplies were in my knapsack. It was an official Girl Scout knapsack that had belonged to my cousin, so I had put masking tape over the logos on both the knapsack and the canteen. The knapsack was kind of small, so I'd had to leave my spare underwear behind. But I was only going to be up there three days. I'd gone a lot longer than that without changing.

Uncle Curtis was a half hour late. When we opened the door, we saw why. "Oh, my poor boys, my poor boys," Grandmother said as she came through the door. She hugged Bobby first and then me as if she would never see us again.

Uncle Curtis sheepishly rubbed the back of his head. "Your grandmother called last night and told me to pick her up."

Mother patted her on the arm. "We'll have breakfast together and then I'll take you home when you want."

"What are you doing up so early, Grandmother?" I asked. She looked rounder than usual. Through the wide collar of her coat, I saw the collars of several additional layers of sweaters.

"I wanted to bring you this," she said. From a bag, she took three small jars with the picture of a pouncing lion. "I can't let you go off without the Lion Salve."

Forget the camping bags and tents— Grandmother had her own survival kit. And it all came in one handy-dandy little container. She swore that stuff would cure most anything.

Uncle Curtis rolled his eyes. "I've brought a first-aid kit, Mama."

Grandmother gathered up all four feet and six inches of her height. "What do you have to keep the damp from weak chests?"

"We're not going camping on a glacier,

Mama," Uncle Curtis said, exasperated.

Grandmother poked him in the chest. "You were always coughing when you were small." And she thrust a jar into his hand.

Mother laughed. "Face it, Curtis. You'll always be her little baby."

"I guess." Uncle Curtis sighed. As he put the jar into his jacket, he kissed Grandmother on the cheek. "Thanks, Mama."

I'd let Grandmother put that gooey stuff on my sore elbow once. Right away the joint had felt hot; and maybe the salve had helped it to heal. However, I stank for two weeks after that.

There was no way I was ever going to use it again. I took a jar and squeezed it into my knapsack. Luckily, it didn't make the knapsack explode.

Grandmother wagged a finger at me. "Promise me you'll use the Lion Salve?"

"We will," Bobby assured her, stowing his carefully away in his pocket.

"And all three of you be sure to wash every day," she added.

"Yes, Grandmother," Bobby and I chorused with Uncle Curtis.

Uncle Curtis tried to get her to sit down, but she insisted on watching as we loaded the gear into Uncle Curtis's old station wagon. There was a heavy canvas tent with its poles, as well as several coolers and lots of other gear. Though the station wagon was as big as a boat, we jammed it full.

"All aboard for the Fun Express, boys!" Uncle Curtis pretended to pull a cord to a locomotive whistle.

"Hey, Curtis, didn't you forget something?" Father teased.

Uncle Curtis ran through his list. "No, I think I've got everything."

"What about this?" Father asked. With his foot, he nudged the ice chest out from behind a chair.

"Right, right," Uncle Curtis brought in a bag of food from the station wagon.

"Careful when you open it up," I warned.

"This is no time for one of your practical jokes." Uncle Curtis glared.

"No, I put dry ice inside instead of regular ice," I said.

"Well," Uncle Curtis said, folding his arms.

"That was good thinking. Now our food should stay cold for the whole trip."

Father patted me on the shoulder. "You did good, boy."

Even Grandmother nodded her head.

"I'm just trying to do my part," I said. This was just the start of my anticlam campaign. I'd show them just how wrong they were about me.

# FIVE ⌃N

**When we had the food** stored away, Grand-mother insisted on one final hug. I was sharp enough to get mine first and then scoot into the front seat beside Uncle Curtis while Grandmother was still squeezing my little brother.

Mother cleared her throat. "Teddy, remember how carsick Bobby gets? He might be better off in the front seat."

I was going to say I had squatter's rights; but then I realized I didn't want Bobby behind me when he was about to throw up. So I wriggled into the backseat where we had stowed more stuff.

The sun was just rising as Uncle Curtis pulled away from the curb.

Grandmother waved a hand and shouted. "No, Curtis, no. The bridge is west. You're going east."

"He's doing it the hard way." Father laughed.

Uncle Curtis turned a bright red as he stopped the car. Rolling down the window, he said, "I know the bridge is west, Mama. I was going around the block."

As he drove on, I twisted around for one final look. Grandmother waved her hand anxiously. After all, we only had three jars of Lion Salve to protect us against the wilderness and all its monsters.

I told myself not to be stupid. I'd been out of Chinatown before to see movies and go to the museum and the park and the zoo. But that had always been for just an afternoon. And I had never been away from San Francisco before.

As the silent buildings rolled by, I began to get this bad feeling in my gut. It was like the one and only time I went on the roller coaster out by Playland. But I told myself not to be stupid. If I turned back now, I'd never change anyone's mind.

Of course, if it had been up to Uncle Curtis, we might have wound up in Disneyland instead.

He and my little brother were busy talking about some nature show they'd both seen the night before. Bobby broke off talking about mountain goats. "Um, Uncle Curtis," he said, "I thought you were going around the block. You're heading south."

"What?" Uncle Curtis peered at a street sign as we passed. "Oh, yeah."

"Do you really get lost looking for the bathroom?" I asked.

"You make a mistake once, and no one ever lets you forget," Uncle Curtis grumbled. "My whole family have memories like elephants."

I would have been just as happy if we had wandered around San Francisco. Bobby, though, was in a hurry to go camping. "Aunt Ethel said you had a map?"

As he turned westward, Uncle Curtis nodded to the glove compartment. "In there. She marked out the route."

"I'll be the navigator then," Bobby volunteered. Opening up the door, he took out the map and unfolded it. "Better make a right turn."

As Uncle Curtis did, he leaned forward to peer

up at the sky. "Funny," he muttered. "The weatherman said it was going to be a hot day."

I leapt in quickly. "All I see are clouds. It looks more like rain." I added hopefully, "Maybe we ought to go back and wait for better weather." No one could blame me for that.

Bobby, though, wasn't going to miss his chance. "It never rains in June," Bobby insisted. "It's a scientific fact!"

Uncle Curtis twitched his thumbs on the steering wheel. "Yeah, well, you can't argue with science. The Fun Express won't stop for a few clouds."

Van Ness was a broad street. On the corner I saw Hippo's, which had all kinds of hamburgers. On the front was a funny drawing of one. The smiling hippo on the sign was my idea of wildlife. And hamburgers beat Spam any day.

Uncle Curtis started talking about another nature show. Again, he got so distracted, we could have continued west into the ocean if Bobby hadn't read the map. Uncle Curtis barely swung his car onto Van Ness in time. Even then, the car behind honked at us.

The sun had risen high enough so that the dark gray clouds hid it. They stretched beyond San Francisco, over the Golden Gate Bridge, and into Marin County. Both the orange bridge towers and the distant hilltops were hidden.

Far below, the waters of the bay were as slick as glass. Here and there a whitecap flawed the smooth green surface.

Ahead of us lay the hills of Marin. They looked as tall and steep as the streets in Chinatown. The colors were all different though. Chinatown had all the colors of a paint store. The Marin hills were just a gold color, like a row of melting butter lumps.

"See the trees on the hills, boys," Uncle Curtis asked, pointing. Here and there were patches of green fur between the hills or low on the slopes. "That's where water collects so trees and bushes can grow."

Bobby announced confidently, "They look like knobcone pines."

Desperately I tried to remember the plants I had read about, but only one stupid plant had stuck in my brain. Even so, I got ready to leap in with it. "Did you know—"

Only, my little brother never gave me the chance. "They need fire to make their cones pop open and drop seeds. That's why wildfires can be good things sometimes." He said it as calmly as if he were commenting on the weather.

"Are you sure about that?" Uncle Curtis asked doubtfully.

"I read it in a library book." Bobby nodded.

"Huh," Uncle Curtis grunted. I was glad to see that I wasn't the only skeptical one. But he didn't argue. My little brother had that effect on people.

Bobby twisted around in the seat to look back at me. "I'm sorry, Teddy. What were you going to say?"

I stared at his face. He was so friendly, so likable. How could I ever compete with that? "Forget it."

Instead, I leaned an elbow against the door. There were cows grazing on the steep, brown hillsides. And suddenly I came up with a nature observation of my own.

"Those hills are as steep as Chinatown hills," I said. "It's a wonder those cows don't break a leg."

Bobby, though, was too excited to pay attention. "Look! A hawk!" Bobby said, pointing. I saw a small black vee circling high in the sky.

"How do you know it's not a seagull that got lost?" I demanded, annoyed.

Uncle Curtis squinted over the wheel. "No, it's too far inland. And look at the shape of its wings. That's got to be a hawk."

Bobby nodded authoritatively. "It's probably a red-tailed hawk."

My uncle and brother watched the hawk, but I just slumped back. Hawk, seagull, or pigeon, it was a bird. And even the hillside cows got boring. Unless Godzilla was stomping on Elsie the cow, I didn't want to see another one.

Bobby, though, didn't get tired at all. Everything made him bounce up and down enthusiastically. Part of me wanted to strangle him just to get him to shut up. However, the other part of me envied him. It must be nice to find the world that exciting.

After a half-hour of brown hillsides and cows, I would have swapped them all for a triple horror feature at the Hub. I guess it was just one more difference between the scientist and the fish-store owner.

The only thing that was interesting was the white globe that Uncle said was an army radar station.

It seemed to take forever before we saw Mount Tamalpais. It rose high above the range of hills like a giant among dwarves. Its slanted sides were brown, too, but spotted with bands of green. You could have put a dozen Chinatowns on its sides. Maybe even San Francisco itself.

Uncle Curtis had been waiting with his own facts. "I bet I know something you don't, Bobby. See the outline?" He lifted his hand from the steering wheel long enough to trace the silhouette. "In the old days, the Native Americans thought the ridgeline was the profile of a sleeping maiden."

Bobby leaned forward. "I see it."

I did my best to see what they saw, but I just couldn't. The ridgeline looked just like a bunch of curves.

"You've been awfully quiet, Teddy. What do you think?" Uncle Curtis asked over his shoulder.

Last year, there had been a new kid who had joined our class. He'd just come from Hong

Kong, and he didn't even know how to catch a ball. In P.E., whenever a ball got thrown to him, his face would screw up with worry.

Now I knew how he felt. It's awful when you can't do what everyone else is doing—especially your little brother. I knew Bobby would keep on trying to help me see the outline if I told them the truth.

I guess if I really wanted to change, I should have asked for help. But I was already tired of being humiliated.

So I just lied, "Yeah, there it is."

I wondered how many more lies I'd pile up before this trip was done. I'd probably set a world record.

# S I X

**Mount Tamalpais kept growing** bigger and bigger as we drove along. I thought some of the skyscrapers in San Francisco had been big, but they were toys compared to it.

You wouldn't think anyone could miss something that huge, but our uncle did. "Look, boys. That hawk's diving!" I thought he had told us everything possible about hawks, but he began spouting more.

"Oh, too bad," Bobby said. "He missed. I wonder what he was going for?"

The hawk wasn't the only one that needed better aim. As we shot past the exit, I leaned over the back of my uncle's seat. "Unh, Uncle Curtis, you should have turned back there."

Bobby rattled his map as he examined it. "Really?"

"Bobby, you're supposed to be the navigator," I sighed.

"I'm sorry," Bobby said.

"How could you miss the sign?" I asked. "It's as big as a car."

"Now, now, no harm." Uncle Curtis shrugged. He left the freeway the first chance he got and then reentered the freeway, heading south.

Bobby leaned against his shoulder strap. "We'll get it this time."

But just as we got near the correct exit, Uncle Curtis suddenly twisted in his seat. "There's a rabbit!" he cried, pointing.

"Where?" Bobby asked, craning his neck.

As we shot past, I moaned, "We missed it again."

Uncle Curtis glanced into the rearview mirror. "Man, that came up faster than I thought."

I put a hand on his shoulder. "Okay. This time, no hawks. No rabbits. Just exit signs. Okay?"

Uncle Curtis gave a thumbs-up. "Got you."

"And don't you dare say anything except navigation stuff," I warned Bobby.

This time we got off at the right exit. I began to wonder how Uncle Curtis found his own bathroom at home. Maybe Aunt Ethel put up signs.

The ranger at the entrance gave us a map of Mount Tamalpais with our campsite marked. "Thanks," Uncle Curtis said. He didn't even glance at it but threw it into the backseat. "I can figure out the way."

The road slanted up steeply and wound round and round the mountain. It seemed to take forever before we pulled into a parking lot on top of the mountain.

Bobby glanced around, puzzled. "Um, Uncle Curtis, I think we've run out of road."

Uncle Curtis rubbed his chin. "Hmm, we must have gone past the campgrounds. I haven't been to this one before."

"It's beautiful up here though," Bobby said, looking around. "It's like we're on top of the world."

However, my stomach was growling. It was insisting that lunch was a lot more important than scenery. I dived into all our gear. It was like mining for coal, but I found the ranger's map.

"Here," I said, passing it over the seat to Uncle Curtis.

He examined it sideways. "I can't make heads or tails out of this crummy map. You'd think with all the taxes we pay, we'd get a better one."

I reached over his shoulder and turned it the correct way. "I think it goes like this." I traced the route back down the road to our campsite.

"Oh, yeah, right," he said, scratching his head. "I see what I did wrong."

But he really didn't. We almost wound up at the ranger's booth again.

If Uncle Curtis was good at one thing, it was making up alibis. I guess he'd had a lot of practice from getting lost all the time. "They really ought to mark the campsite better," he grumbled.

"Well, we're getting to see a lot of the mountain," Bobby said. He was always trying to find the silver lining.

Big deal. I would rather have had a meal. "Let me help," I said. I took the map from Uncle Curtis. "Just drive slowly."

I managed to get us to the parking lot of the campgrounds. Tents dotted the slope under the trees like a rag quilt.

"It's crowded," I said. With a little luck, someone would have taken our reserved spot.

"But none of them are on the Fun Express," Uncle Curtis insisted. When he had parked, he took the map from me and jumped out of the car. "This way, boys, for the beginning of your great adventure."

We followed him up a dirt trail from the parking lot to a patch by some trees. Uncle Curtis stopped. "This is it," he declared, folding the map into neat little squares. "The great outdoors!"

As I kicked at one of the many rocks on the ground, I didn't see what was so great about it. "Isn't fun supposed to be less lumpy?"

My parents are always scolding me about being so messy. However, they should have seen Mother Nature. There were all these pebbles and leaves littering the dirt. I would have tidied up a little, especially for paying guests.

Satisfied, Uncle Curtis surveyed the site. "All this fresh air! It's guaranteed to make you feel so tired, you won't notice any rocks."

I think you could get just as tired breathing bus fumes. However, I kept my mouth shut and helped unload the station wagon. Though it was a cloudy day, it was still warm and muggy. Almost everyone was in T-shirts and shorts. However, Bobby and I were wearing our usual clothes for a San Francisco summer: sweatshirts and corduroy pants. The corduroy made a flapping sound when the trouser legs rubbed together.

Soon we were both sweating. In San Francisco, the thermostat was set to a sensible sixty degrees or so. Not like this oven. So finally we took off our sweatshirts and tied the sleeves around our waists.

I was glad Grandmother wasn't around. She would have made us keep them on, so we wouldn't catch cold.

As we worked, dust got into everything. It was all over my clothes. It was in my mouth. I felt like I was being buried alive.

It didn't seem to bother Uncle Curtis, though. He was humming happily as he unrolled the army surplus tent. Then he laid out the tent stakes where he wanted them. Finally, he took out an army shovel with a short handle. Unfolding it, he put it together quickly.

"Now I'll demonstrate the fine art of putting up a tent," he said. Kneeling, he used the flat of the shovel blade to hammer the stake into the ground.

"Me next," Bobby said eagerly.

"You want to try everything, don't you?" Uncle Curtis grinned, but he surrendered the shovel.

I knew my little brother, so I stepped back. Bobby thought that energy could always make up for lack of coordination. Uncle Curtis, though, made the mistake of staying close to supervise. He almost lost a kneecap when Bobby whacked at the tent stake and missed.

"Easy there," Uncle Curtis warned as he stumbled back.

Most of the time I try to get someone else to do all the work. But I saw another chance to prove I was just as good as my little brother.

"Let me have a turn," I said, holding out my hand.

I guess Uncle Curtis figured Bobby could take forever. "Let Teddy do that. You help me get the tent ready."

"But I want to do it," Bobby complained.

Uncle Curtis rubbed his head. "The sooner we set up camp, the sooner I can show you around. Isn't that what's really important?"

Bobby grudgingly handed the shovel to me and helped Uncle Curtis unroll the tent itself.

The ground was a lot harder than it looked. But lifting all those boxes in the store had given me muscles. So I hammered away until I got the stakes in.

It took all three of us to put up the tent. I still thought it leaned a little when we were done.

Uncle Curtis inspected the tent ropes carefully. He acted as though they were the cables holding up the Golden Gate Bridge. Finally, though, he nodded his head in approval. "That looks good."

When we had stowed our gear inside, I said, "I'm hungry. Let's eat."

"We've gotten used to eating Spam," Bobby explained.

"When you ride the Fun Express, you dine first class," Uncle Curtis boasted as he went over to the ice chest in the shadow of a big tree. He squatted down and undid the lid's clasps. "I brought hot dogs and hamburgers. I'll make you boys a feast."

When he raised the lid, fog rolled out around him.

Bobby and I jumped back. "What's wrong?" my brother asked.

"It's just the dry ice." I laughed. I was enjoying my moment of triumph.

Uncle Curtis fanned his hand over the chest to help blow away some of the fog. "Boy, Teddy, I know this is one batch of meat that's not going to spoil."

White ribbons crept out of the chest and down the sides while Uncle Curtis carefully lifted out a big parcel wrapped in pink butcher paper.

He lost his grin though. "It's like a glacier."

I poked at the package in his hands. It was cold enough to make my body and hands ache. Through the paper, I traced the shape of hot dogs. "They feel like rocks."

Uncle Curtis lifted out the other package and hefted it over his shoulder like a shot put. "The hamburger's like a lump of coal, too."

I wasn't going to let this ruin my achievement. "Let's set them out," I urged. "Part of one of these packages will thaw out and we can have that."

So Uncle Curtis placed both packages out on a rock. "You boys have to get some firewood anyway. Just pick up the dead wood lying around. We're not allowed to chop down any trees."

"Right away," Bobby said, heading out.

"Wait for me, oh, fearless leader," I muttered, and wandered off after Bobby. "Just how much wood do you need to cook food anyway?" I asked the researcher. "I don't think we can carry back a log."

"The books didn't say," Bobby said, "but on television they always seem to use wood about this thick." He held his fingers apart about six inches.

In the movies, there's always dead wood lying around, but all we could gather were twigs.

Disgusted, I looked at the handful I had. "This isn't even enough for a broom."

Bobby held up his own. "The other campers must have picked the mountain clean."

When we returned, Uncle Curtis stared at the handfuls of twigs. "That's okay for kindling. But where are the branches?"

"This is all we could find," I confessed helplessly.

Uncle Curtis rubbed the back of his neck. "I was counting on using firewood."

I saw a column of smoke rising a short distance away. "Maybe someone has spare firewood?"

"I'll borrow some. Nature lovers always share with one another. It's the code of camping," Uncle Curtis said. Suddenly he slapped himself. "Ow. Darn mosquitoes."

Apparently, there were other creatures besides humans having a meal. "I guess it's time to use my birthday gift," I said.

I went back to the tent. Something rustled in the brush nearby, but the bushes were too small for a bear to hide behind. So I went inside and got the mosquito repellent.

I can't say it did much good. Even as I sprayed my arm, a mosquito flew right through the mist to land on it. "This stuff just makes us tastier to the mosquitoes," I said.

I was hot, sweaty, being eaten alive, and hungry. So hungry that even Spam would have tasted good.

I poked each package in disappointment. "They're still like ice."

Bobby turned the packages over on the rock. They each clonked against the stone. "Darn dry ice." Frustrated, he picked up the package and dropped it against the rock. It landed with a loud crack. I thought there was a fifty-fifty chance that either the rock or the meat had broken.

Uncle Curtis grabbed a package under either arm. "We'll defrost the meat as we cook it. What's the menu for today, boys? Hot dogs or hamburgers?"

Bobby punched cheerfully at the air. "Hot dogs!"

I guess the dry ice hadn't been such a good idea, after all. Sulking, I jammed my hands in my pockets. "I'll settle for anything that isn't part of the polar ice cap."

Uncle Curtis put the hamburger into the chest and snapped the clasps shut. "You boys bring the buns and mess kits. I'll bring the hot dogs."

The cooking area was an open space. A row of stoves had been built from stones and metal grills.

Uncle Curtis went over to a table where some campers were eating.

He came back with half a bag of charcoal. "Ten dollars for this," he complained. "Fellow lovers of nature, my eye."

"Well, maybe it's the membership fee to the club," I said.

Uncle Curtis shot me a dirty look as he poured charcoal from the bag into the pit beneath the metal grill. Without lighter fluid, it took a little work and a lot of fanning and blowing before the coals caught.

As the coals slowly turned red, we began to set our stuff out on a nearby picnic table.

The previous cooks had not bothered to clean the grill. Uncle Curtis, though, had brought a spatula. He used it to scrape the metal bars.

In the meantime, we unwrapped the paper. The hot dogs were fused together into a lump the size of a football. No matter how hard we tried, we could not break them apart.

"Wait." Bobby proudly opened his borrowed mess kit and took out a fork. When he tried to pry a hot dog off, the tines bent.

We still hadn't freed any hot dogs by the time the coals were ready. By now, Uncle Curtis was too impatient to be careful. Lifting the mass of hot dogs, he set the whole fused lump on the grill. "I'll pry them off as they defrost." Water began dripping onto the coals with loud hisses. As steam rose around the hot dogs, Uncle Curtis straightened the tines of the fork. Carefully he worked at one of the hot dogs. "Almost . . . almost," he muttered.

With a plop, the hot dog fell through the grill and onto the coals. In no time, it was as black as a stick of charcoal. By the time this had happened to three more hot dogs, I tried to use a stick to ease them out of the coals.

Uncle Curtis shoved me back. "They're dirty."

"I don't care," I admitted. "I'm hungry."

"And they're half raw, too." He threw them into a trash can.

We were still trying to defrost the hot dogs long after the other campers had left. What wasn't burnt into charcoal was like a Popsicle. "We could get worms from eating raw meat." Uncle Curtis sighed. "And then what would your grandmother say? We'll eat the marshmallows instead."

We took the meat-cicles back with us, expecting them to defrost by dinnertime. "We can put the marshmallows on the sticks you brought back," Uncle Curtis said. "And then we can heat them over the coals."

That cheered me up a little. No meal can be too bad if it's mostly sugar.

"They should be in a paper sack, Teddy," Uncle Curtis said as he put the hot dogs back on the rock.

As I went to the tent, I saw its sides moving. I figured it was just the wind, but when I raised the flap of the tent, a gray furry bundle waddled out.

It was about the size of a watermelon, but covered all over with gray fur. On its face it had a black mask. From television, I knew it was a raccoon.

Calmly it licked a sticky paw. His toes looked a lot like little fingers.

"Aren't you supposed to be scared of me?" I asked him. Animals always were, on the nature shows.

I thought I saw him shrug. Then he cleaned the other paw.

"Well, I'm bigger than you," I pointed out to him. "That should count for something."

With a sniff, he strolled away into the brush.

I watched him disappear. Then, curious, I raised the flap on the tent.

Inside it was a mess—even worse than my part of our bedroom at home. The sleeping bags had been tumbled about. Worse, the paper bags had been torn open.

Suddenly I understood why the raccoon had licked his paws. The plastic sack with the marshmallows had been split apart. Only a few marshmallows were left. They lay scattered in the dirt.

I whirled around. The brush was still shaking in the distance.

"You rotten little pig. I hope you get cavities," I yelled.

# SEVEN 🌲⛰

**Worried, I checked my knapsack next.** My good-ies were still safe. I guess the raccoon preferred American snacks to Chinese ones. Or maybe I'd stopped him before he got to the next course.

I was hungry enough to toss my snacks all down in one gulp. After all, we were in the wilderness, weren't we? In the wilderness, it's the survival of the fittest. I'd learned that much from Bobby's nature shows. The Daniel Boones outside could have the preserved plums.

Surprisingly, that was when my conscience reared its head. I figured it had stayed back in Chinatown where it was comfortable. But it had come along to poke and prod me. After all, it was my fault we couldn't have hot dogs or hamburgers yet.

My conscience didn't win often, but it picked a day when I was tired from getting up early.

With a sigh, I slung my knapsack over one shoulder and hauled it up to the stove. Then I broke the bad news. I'd expected them to feel as bad as I did. Maybe they'd even be willing to go home before we starved to death.

I should have known better.

"A raccoon!" Teddy said happily. "Lucky!" Only my little brother would enjoy a raccoon's company. "Tell me all about him."

"He was an animal." I shrugged. Beasts were Bobby's interests, not mine. "But he wasn't shy at all."

"Maybe it's because we're on his territory," Bobby said, rubbing his chin. "And if he sees humans all the time, he might lose his natural fear."

I opened my knapsack. "I brought along some snacks. We can share."

Uncle Curtis took a strip of coconut candy and held it between his fingers. "We left Chinatown so we could get away from this kind of stuff."

I wished I was back there now. Then I could get

a decent lunch. "You can get hot dogs and hamburgers in Chinatown, too," I said.

Bobby laid ginger candy inside a bun. He was always trying to make lemonade out of lemons. "Maybe we'll invent a new sandwich. Then we can make lots of money."

"And buy a yacht," Uncle Curtis agreed, copying him.

I did the same. When I tried my ginger sandwich, though, I knew we wouldn't have to worry about getting rich. Uncle Curtis just began eating out of the paper sacks like me. Even Bobby gave up on the bread.

We munched away at what we could while the wildlife began to munch on us.

Bobby was about halfway through his sandwich when he slapped at his arm. "It's a mosquito. I would have thought the smoke by the stoves would keep them away."

"It must be one of the tough ones," Uncle Curtis said. The next second he slapped his cheek. Bobby's attacker had pals.

Then I felt something bite my wrist. I slapped at it too late. By the end of lunch, we all had mosquito bites. Bobby had little lumps all over his face and hands. Even he found it hard to find something good to say about the mosquitoes. "How come they bite me so much?"

"You must be the tastiest," Uncle Curtis said. Standing up, he stretched. "I guess it's too late to go for a real hike."

"We still have to defrost the hamburger," I protested. "We have to keep an eye on it. Otherwise, the raccoon will get it when it thaws out."

"Can't we go for a short walk at least?" Bobby begged.

"Curtis's Fun Express never stops." Uncle Curtis nodded, putting the hot dogs back into the chest.

We brought our stuff back to the tent, and I showed them the damage. Bobby was more interested in the tracks though. He studied the space between them. "It must have been big."

"Like a hassock with legs," I said. Maybe it had been a good thing I hadn't caught the raccoon after all.

Uncle Curtis turned in a slow circle. "I thought I saw a trail near here."

"I think it's there," Bobby said, pointing to our left.

We walked past the other tents. I didn't see anyone else though. I guess they were all off enjoying nature. Back home, I could have been watching a triple feature at the Hub.

The trail head was a hundred yards away. Pale gray-green bushes grew on either side. The narrow dirt path snaked through the high brush. A couple of nature lovers came around a bend. They had deep tans and wore kerchiefs around their necks. And they bounced energetically as they walked. They nodded and smiled as they passed us.

I looked at the tall bushes with the small, bright green leaves. They looked like they were cut out of leather. "Golden Gate Park has better plants," I said. "And it's awfully messy here." In fact, it reminded me of the time when the park gardeners went on strike. *And* at least in Golden Gate Park, there were snack stands.

"We're in an area of chaparral," Uncle Curtis explained. "It's past the season to see blooms. It's so dry in the summer that the plants are at rest instead."

As for the animals, I heard a single bird, and that was it. Uncle Curtis and Bobby got into a deep discussion about whether it was a thrasher or something else. They both agreed that it would be easier to identify it if we could see it. For all we knew, some hidden ranger could be playing a tape.

Aside from the raccoon, I saw more animal life in Chinatown. There always some pigeon, gull, or rat scavenging in the garbage cans. So I got pretty bored.

That didn't stop Bobby and Uncle Curtis, though. They examined twigs, rocks, and even the dirt. Our uncle must have been watching a lot of nature shows, too. It was just like him to treat camping like homework. However, he still didn't know as much as my little brother.

Again, I tried to remember the book I had read. All I could remember, though, was that one dumb plant. Even so, I got ready to spring it on them. I wanted to impress them with my learning.

I was so busy repeating my memorized lesson to myself that I almost bumped into their backs.

The pair of them had stopped dead before some

big sunny rocks. "I thought I saw something," Uncle Curtis said. He squatted down, peering this way and that.

"There," Bobby said, jabbing his finger excitedly. I saw some dirt and pebbles fall from a crevice. "The snake went in there."

"Snake?" I asked. I started to look around for a weapon to defend us.

My little brother, though, began circling the rock. "Yeah."

Snatching up a stick, I swung it up like a bat. "Stand back. I won't let that rattler get you."

Uncle Curtis leaned over the stones. "Relax, Teddy. It's just a harmless little garter snake. I bet they love these rocks."

Great. A housing project for serpents.

All snakes gave me the heebie-jeebies. I was ready to head back to camp, but Bobby and Uncle Curtis kept hovering. They wanted a glimpse of the garter snake. I was worried, though, that some of its cousins might come for a visit. Cousins with rattles.

I was practically jumping out of my skin by the time they gave up. Only we didn't head back to camp like I wanted. Against my better judgment, we charged on.

Bobby was so happy that he didn't pay any attention to me. But Uncle Curtis noticed.

While Bobby was examining a bug, he asked me, "What's the matter, Teddy? You're dragging your feet."

I didn't want to give him an excuse to scold me. "I'm just feeling sort of tired. We got up awfully early."

Uncle Curtis scratched his cheek. "Yeah, I know. But I wanted to make sure you had enough time on the Fun Express. Look, Teddy. You won't see this in Chinatown." And he plunged off the trail and waded through the dense leaves that covered the ground. "Now, look at the leaves on this tree."

"Sure," Bobby said.

Suddenly I noticed my plant. It was my big chance. So, stopping Bobby, I cleared my throat.

"In a moment, Teddy." Uncle Curtis smiled patiently.

"But—" I began.

"Let me finish," Uncle Curtis insisted. "The

leaves are that way so the plant won't lose its moisture in the summer heat."

My parents and my grandmother were always telling me to respect my elders. So I shut up and listened to Uncle Curtis go on and on about tree leaves.

When he finished, he gave me a friendly nod. "Okay, Teddy, what is it?"

"You're standing in poison oak," I said, and pointed at the green leaves all around Uncle Curtis's ankles.

I hadn't realized Uncle Curtis could move that fast—or jump that far. When he was back on the path, he started to reach down.

"The oil from the leaves might still be on your shoes," I warned.

Uncle Curtis didn't seem too happy about that bit of knowledge. "You don't say?" He did his best to wipe the sides of his shoes in the dirt. Then he glanced at his watch. "Well, I guess the meat should be defrosted by now."

I think he wanted to wash off his shoes. I just wanted to get away from the snake apartments.

So we turned around. When we reached the end

of the trail, however, we were at a road. "I don't remember a fork in the trail," Uncle Curtis said, scratching his head.

Fortunately, at that moment a tanned couple passed us on the path. "Excuse us," they said.

"Are you going back to the campgrounds?" I asked them.

"That's right," the man grinned.

I grabbed Bobby's hand. "Let's follow them."

When we reached our tent, I saw the canvas sides rustling once more. "Not again," I said as I rushed forward.

"Neat-o," Bobby said, darting after me.

"Wait right here, boys," Uncle Curtis said, catching us. "You have to be cautious with any wild animal."

"But he's going through our stuff again," I protested.

"Just make some noise. He'll leave," Uncle Curtis said to me and then shouted at the tent, "Shoo! Shoo!"

The raccoon waddled out of the tent. He stared at us indignantly. I guess he had been expecting us to set out another meal for him.

Bobby squatted down and held out a hand in invitation. "Hello, boy. Over here."

The raccoon looked down its snout at my little brother. Then the animal turned his back on us and strutted away.

Bobby was hopping up and down with joy. "Wasn't that neat-o?" he asked me.

"Animals sometimes follow a set pattern during the day," Uncle Curtis said thoughtfully. "I wonder if we pitched our tent on one of his trails."

I just groaned. "Great. Right on top of a raccoon freeway."

"Then we'll get to see a lot more of him," my little brother said excitedly.

"We'll have to keep an eye on the meat, or the raccoon will steal that, too," I pointed out.

"Right. We can take turns guarding it," Uncle Curtis said. "Let's try the hamburger this time." Taking it out of the cooler, he set it on a rock to thaw beside the hot dogs.

I hoped it would melt enough in the next few hours. All we had left were buns and salted plums. And I was still so hungry.

I didn't see how things could get any worse,

when I felt something wet on top of my head. I looked up to see if it came from a bird. And I got a drop of water straight in my eye.

A raindrop splattered on the ground. It made a small dark circle by my shoe. And then there was another.

And then a whole bunch came pattering down.

# EIGHT 🍁

**By the time we got to the tent,** we were as soggy as sponges.

"It never rains in June," Uncle Curtis grumbled. He'd taken off his shoes and socks with a rag from the station wagon and left them out so the storm could wash off the poison-oak oil.

I listened to the rain drumming on the tent canvas. "You should tell the clouds that."

Uncle Curtis lifted the flap. The rain was falling hard. It was like being under a waterfall. "And there's no sign of it letting up soon." He lowered the flap. "But at least we have shelter. Good job, boys."

"Teddy did most of it," Bobby said.

"I was glad to do something good for a change," I mumbled. I was bombing at outsmarting Bobby. At least I had more muscles than he did. For now, I'd have to be satisfied with that.

"We should change into dry clothes," Uncle Curtis said, reaching for his pack.

"I left my spares at home," I confessed. "The knapsack was so small, and I needed room for the snacks."

"Well, it's a good thing you did," Uncle Curtis admitted. "Here, you can have mine."

"I brought extras," Bobby said.

Somehow I managed to squeeze into some of Bobby's stuff. Instead of putting on the other set, Bobby rooted around in his backpack.

"Better put something dry on," I warned him.

"The coldness could get into our chests." He took out his little jar of Lion Salve. It was like him to remember Grandmother's advice.

I tried to snatch it from him. "That will stink up the joint."

Bobby nodded at my bare feet. "It won't be any worse than those." Unscrewing the cap, he began smearing the salve on his chest.

Uncle Curtis shook his head. "You're supposed to use it for aches and pains."

"We promised Grandmother, after all." Bobby kept slapping on layer after layer.

I stared at Bobby in disbelief. "Why don't you just get a paint roller?"

He wiggled around so his back was to us. "Will one of you guys get my shoulder blades? I can't reach them."

"Unh-unh. I'm not touching that gunk," Uncle Curtis said. "It takes weeks to get rid of the smell." He gave a cough. By now, with his layers of Lion Salve, Bobby was . . . well, pungent.

Bobby twisted around toward me. "Teddy, will you help?"

"Forget it." I unrolled my sleeping bag and then peered inside. When I didn't see any snakes, I burrowed into it. I tried to cover my nose with the material.

Grumbling, Bobby wrapped his arms around himself. He wriggled and twisted like an eel with arms. Finally, every square inch of his skin was protected. "Woo-hoo," he said, wiggling around as the Lion Salve took effect. "I feel like a chili pepper." It always felt hot at first.

He was so slick he almost slid back into his T-shirt. I watched him restore layer after layer of clothing. Even so, the scent of Lion Salve penetrated the tent, sleeping bags, and everything else. Screwing the lid back on, he returned it to his pack.

Then, snug in his protective vapors, Bobby spread his sleeping bag on the ground. Taking a book from his bag, he began to read.

Holding his sleeping bag up around his shoulders, Uncle Curtis crawled like a green slug over to me.

"Tomorrow we steal the Lion Salve," he whispered to me, "and bury it somewhere."

I grinned. For once, I could agree with Uncle.

"At least the Lion Salve should keep any critters away tonight," Uncle Curtis muttered, wrinkling his nose.

I coughed again. "They'll stay away if they don't want to suffocate."

I gave a jump when I heard a loud crack outside. "What's that?"

Uncle Curtis lifted the flap and looked around in the gray, misty air. "A branch fell down."

"We'll have firewood then," I said, shivering in the draft through the opening.

"We might be able to break off some of it," he agreed. He dropped the flap.

I tried to sleep, but the Lion Salve choked the air.

Suddenly I felt a crawling sensation on my forehead. I slapped my forehead and my hand felt wet.

I sat up on one elbow. A line of ants crawled through the tent and right over the sleeping bags. I swatted and crushed, but the ants kept coming.

In desperation, I got out of my bag and turned it upside down. I was so busy with the ants that I wound up stepping on someone's foot.

"Ow! Watch out, clumsy," Uncle Curtis complained.

A new stinking cloud of Lion Salve wafted over me, so I figured it had to be Bobby sitting up. "Sorry," I said.

At that moment, the blackness descended with a loud flap. Frightened, I tried to shove it away, but it was everywhere. It hung on my head and hands. At any moment, I expected it to start choking me. The others thrashed around, too.

The blackness was not heavy, but it was steady.

It just would not go away as it tried to flatten us. I wound up on my stomach. Desperately I began to crawl. Suddenly, my head broke into the open air.

"Help, help!" Bobby was crying, and I heard a thud.

I dragged myself to freedom. Then I turned around in the rain. Under the canvas, I saw two shapes weaving and bobbing. Then I realized they were just my tentmates, trapped underneath our tent.

I began hauling at the canvas. "It's just the tent," I reassured them. "It fell down."

Bobby was the first to creep out. Then Uncle Curtis. His face was flushed bright red, his eyes were still wide with fear, and he was panting as if he had run a mile.

He sat down in the mud. "You'd think I'd know how to tie a knot to keep a tent up," Uncle Curtis admitted.

Bobby held up one of the stakes. "No, see? The rope's still tied to the stake."

"Then it's my fault," I said. "I didn't drive the stakes in far enough. Some muscles I have." I felt like crawling back under the tent and hiding. It seemed like every time I tried to do something better than Bobby, I failed.

Bobby peered under the canvas. "At least the ground's still dry under the canvas."

"Even if we aren't," I said.

Uncle Curtis turned. "We can use that tree branch to prop up the middle temporarily." He went over to a tree and came back dragging a branch behind him. It was a couple of yards long. That must have been the thing that made the thud.

He bent and then broke the side branches from the main one. Finally he had a more or less straight pole. Pulling it behind him, he disappeared under the canvas once more. The next moment the middle of the tent began to rise upward. "Come inside out of that rain, boys. It'll be a little snug, but you won't get as wet this way."

When I raised the flap, I saw Uncle Curtis squatting in the center of the tent. He was holding the pole up himself.

"We can take turns," I offered.

"No, this trip was my idea. I'll do it," he said stubbornly. "Get into your sleeping bags, boys, and try to stay warm."

Uncle Curtis might give lousy presents, but you could always count on him to do the right thing. And maybe that was just as important.

I went under the canvas, groping for my sleeping bag. When I found it, I slapped it. Maybe that would scare the snakes away.

"Some camping trip this is," our human tent pole said to us. "I'm sorry, boys. Do you want to go home?"

Those were the words I had been hoping for. However, Bobby spoke up before I could. "You couldn't help it about the rain."

I could have cheerfully kicked Bobby right then. I couldn't chicken out while he wanted to stay.

"No," I said, "it's okay."

But as I lay in my sleeping bag, I played the only-child game again.

# NINE

**The rain let up by dinnertime.** We slogged over to the hamburger. The soggy paper had fallen off the hamburger, which was still as hard as a red meteorite, and the hot dogs were just as bad.

When I made a mistake, I didn't make a small one. I made one as big as a mountain.

Uncle Curtis rapped a knuckle against the meat. "Maybe you could use this as a doorstop, Teddy."

Red-faced, I offered one of the paper bags. "Salted plums, anyone?"

Uncle Curtis pulled out his wallet with a sigh. "I won't let you boys starve." He shuffled off through the mud. Still barefoot, he slipped a couple of times but managed to catch his balance.

He came back a short while later with a couple of cans of beans. "Beans and buns aren't bad." It was more of a question than a statement.

I didn't want to make him feel bad. "No, that's great. But how much did it cost?"

"You don't want to know," he winced.

"I think the can opener's inside the tent," Bobby said. It had collapsed when we let go of the branch.

Uncle Curtis set the cans down. "We should set the tent back up anyway while it's still light."

I thought it wouldn't take as long, because this time Bobby and I knew what we were doing. Wet canvas weighs about twice as much, however. At least it was easier to drive the stakes into the wet dirt. This time I made sure to smash them in solid.

Uncle Curtis was unusually quiet. Even though he'd gotten me into this muddy mess, I felt kind of sorry for him, so I tried to make conversation.

"How'd you learn about camping, Uncle Curtis?" I asked. I know Father and Uncle Mat had gone camping with Uncle Curtis a couple of times.

"In the army," he said. "Military service isn't

like the movies, you know. I hated every minute of it—except the camping."

"Even though there's mud and bugs and raccoons?" I asked.

Uncle Curtis paused in the middle of tying a knot. "I like it because of them. What do you see when you look at me, Teddy?"

"My uncle Curtis," I said. I didn't add that he could be pretty picky sometimes.

A corner of his mouth curled up. "Thanks for being nice. But what do you see when you look at me?"

My arms were getting tired holding the rope that held up a corner of the tent. I wished he'd finish tying the knot. "My uncle Curtis."

He shrugged. "You mean, you see a middle-aged guy who's getting chubby. I sit at a desk all day. I pay my bills. I take care of my family. I do the same routine day in and day out. In other words, safe but boring."

I thought of what Father had said. That was the clam's life to a T. I hadn't known he'd felt the same as me. "You don't like it?" I asked.

"No," Uncle Curtis said softly. "Even when I

was a kid, people thought I was a real yawner. So back then I started trying to show I was more." He studied his bare feet. "But all I ever do is make everyone think I'm just a stuffed shirt who talks too much." He was a lot sharper than I thought.

"If you know what you're doing, why don't you stop?" I asked.

He grinned with one side of his mouth. "Don't you think I try? But I can't help it. I guess I've been doing it too long."

I felt so sorry for him. "You're not so bad," I said. I never thought I would tell Uncle Curtis that.

"Well." He sighed. "It's just the way I am. I've done the best with what I had, but I didn't have your opportunities. You and Bobby can have the whole world now."

So he wanted the same thing for me that I did. I hesitated, but then I said softly, "I'd . . . I'd like that." That's more than I'd ever admitted to anyone else. And then I waited for him to rib me like Uncle Mat or Father.

Uncle Curtis studied me. "Really? I wasn't sure."

I wondered what he had been like when he was

my age. Had his father told him what mine had told me?

"It's not that I don't like Chinatown," I said.

"No, of course not," Uncle Curtis agreed. "Chinatown will always be my home, and I'll always want to go back to it." His cold fingers worked stiffly at the knot for a moment. "It's just that life should be about change. Otherwise you feel trapped." He wriggled his own shoulders as if something was pushing down on them.

"I don't know what you mean," I said.

"Is it like hermit crabs? They have to find new shells," Bobby said. "They outgrow the old one. So they have to find a new one."

Uncle Curtis nodded. "I want to keep growing. I don't want to play it safe in Chinatown."

I stared at Uncle Curtis. I had always thought I knew him. What had happened to my fussy, boring uncle?

"So that's why you go camping?" I asked cautiously.

Uncle Curtis tugged at the end of the rope. "I guess I'm running out of camping buddies. Nancy and Ethel quit after one time. Your father and

Uncle Mat bailed out, too."

He sounded a little lonesome.

"I'll always come with you," Bobby promised.

I thought over what he had said. He was a fellow clam, after all, who wanted to be more—just like me. "Well, maybe you're right," I admitted. "I ought to get out of Chinatown every now and then. I'm just not sure that camping is how I want to do it."

Frustrated, he ran a hand through his hair. "You're as hardheaded as Nancy. She acted like I was punishing her."

That made me a little uncomfortable. Who wanted to be like my fussy cousin? "Well . . . unh . . . thanks for bringing us up here. I guess you meant well."

"Look, Teddy. I'll just ask you for this: Give the Fun Express one last chance," Uncle Curtis said, and then suddenly he slapped his cheek. "Ow. These darn mosquitoes. They're making up for meals they lost during the rain."

There were buzzing little specks all around us now. I slapped at one on my leg. "There's even more of them than before."

Uncle Curtis and I were both waving our hands

like windmills. Bobby, though, was just standing there. His eyes darted this way and that as he watched the mosquitoes. His face had a dreamy expression. He always looked that way when he was being a scientist. "They change direction so fast." If he hadn't been holding a rope, he probably would have been writing notes.

"The mosquitoes were eating you alive before this," I said, annoyed. "What happened?"

Uncle Curtis had been watching Bobby. "They don't want to get within a foot of you. But we used the same mosquito repellent. It doesn't make any sense."

"Maybe I got un-tasty somehow," Bobby suggested. His eyes still followed the flight of an insect.

I sniffed at him, catching a whiff of the familiar odor. "It's the Lion Salve."

"Just wait till the company hears that." Uncle Curtis laughed. "I can't wait to hear their new ads."

Despite everything, I had to chuckle. "Forget the ads. I can't wait to hear Grandmother."

When we were done setting up the tent, Uncle

Curtis triple-checked all the knots and stakes. He wasn't going to have the tent fall again. If anything, we'd have problems striking the tent.

Then we went inside and smeared Lion Salve on ourselves. When I stepped back outside, I had to laugh. The mosquitoes swirled all around me, but none of them wanted to go near me. I felt like I was wearing invisible armor.

"I guess mosquitoes hate Lion Salve even more than I do." I laughed.

Uncle Curtis scratched an ankle. "I just wish it worked on poison oak. I think some got through my socks."

# TEN

**Uncle Curtis rapped the hamburger** and hot dogs with a knuckle and then shook his head. "They're still solid as a rock. I guess we'll try again tomorrow."

The blood rushed to my cheeks. "Sorry," I said. "I guess it wasn't such a hot idea, after all."

Uncle Curtis, who'd gotten a pair of old sneakers from the station wagon, cradled our meat-cicles in one arm. Then he used his free hand to pretend to straight-arm someone. "I guess we could always play football. I just wouldn't try to punt."

I stared at him. He was always so serious. I hardly ever remember him telling a joke. He was straight-faced, though, as he opened the chest. Frosty ribbons drifted up like snakes.

"There's still a lot of dry ice left," Bobby said. He leaned over to peer at it.

Uncle Curtis held Bobby back with his free hand. "I think only I should handle the dry ice, Mr. Scientist."

Bobby looked disappointed and ready to argue. However, I was more worried about my stomach than science. "What if the hamburger or hot dogs don't defrost?"

"Don't worry. I won't let you boys starve." Locking the lid, he straightened up. "Bring the wet clothes, too, boys. We'll dry them by the stove."

I eyed his contaminated shoes and socks. "Should we bring those too?"

"Leave them," Uncle Curtis said. "Anyone who takes them is in for a nasty surprise."

I just hoped that "anyone" would be the raccoon.

We tried to break up the branch Uncle Curtis had been using as a tent pole; but the wood was so green it wouldn't snap, so we gave up. That still left us with a lot of stuff to carry up to the cooking stoves. As we walked through the campground, we saw a lot of unhappy, muddy people around. Some of them were already packing up their wet tents and gear.

The mosquitoes didn't help the spirits of the other campers, either. Everyone was slapping themselves as if they were doing some strange dance. However, thanks to Grandmother's Lion Salve, we were wallflowers now. You just didn't want to get near us. But at least we were mosquito-proof.

Of course, the stoves were wet, so poor Uncle Curtis had to buy some lighter fluid. "My wallet's getting a lot flatter from this trip," he joked.

It would have been cheaper for him if he had bought me another bird-watching guide for my birthday.

Soon, though, the buns were toasted, and the beans were bubbling in the cans. And we were warming and drying ourselves and our spare clothes by the heat. Uncle Curtis kept an eagle eye to make sure that we didn't get too close, though.

He was pretty cheery when he finally spooned the beans out onto the buns. "Chow time, boys."

We took our food over to one of the picnic tables and sat down. I poked at the pile of beans in the brown gravy. At home, I always hated them. And yet they smelled good right now. So I put a forkful into my mouth. "These are delicious! What brand is this?" I asked, looking at the label of one of them. "I want to get more."

Uncle Curtis grinned. "Well, don't be surprised if it doesn't taste the same at home. It's the outdoors. It always makes food tastier."

We wolfed down what we had cooked and then cleaned up the area. I was feeling a lot better, too. A full stomach will do that.

The sun was going down as we headed back down. In the dimming light, we took small steps on the slippery trail. Uncle Curtis was limping as if some of the poison oak had really gotten on his ankles after all and was bothering him now. Lanterns glowed inside the tents. They looked like living, glowing mushrooms now.

We got back to our camp as the sun set. The clouds covered the sky except for a narrow band on the horizon. The sky around the sun glowed a bright orange. And so did the clouds just above it. The further you looked, though, the more the clouds darkened until they were a deep purple.

"That's awfully pretty," Bobby said.

"I just wish the sky had been clear." Uncle Curtis sighed. "It would have been even prettier for you boys. I hope you're not disappointed."

Camping would still not be my pick for a birthday present. But Uncle Curtis really thought he was doing something that would please us. And that was not such a bad thing.

I started to shiver. As hot as it had been in the daytime, it was already getting chilly. So I wound up putting on all my clothes. Most of them were pretty dry by now.

Uncle Curtis and Bobby copied me. Then Uncle Curtis brought out his big flashlight. "Now it's time for the scary stories."

"Can't we just tell jokes?" Bobby asked. Bobby hated anything scary.

I shook my head determinedly. "All you know are knock-knock jokes. And I've heard all of those a hundred times."

"Besides," Uncle Curtis said, "the outdoors

always makes scary stories scarier, just as it makes food tastier."

"Oh," Bobby said in a small voice, "if those are the rules."

"They are," I said smugly. I'd seen every horror and monster movie. Storytelling was one thing I could do better than Bobby. I could tell the plot of those movies. And I bet I'd frighten Bobby so bad that he wouldn't dare sleep tonight. (After all, big brothers have to help toughen up little brothers.)

I sat down on a rock. "Well, I saw this movie just last week," I said. "See, there was this guy. . . ." I told them about Snake Man Two. Soon Bobby was on the edge of his rock listening. "And then he heard this noise," I said, finishing. "*Sss, sss, sssss.* He heard it slithering closer and closer. And then his match went out!

"And," I said, "the snake man struck!" Reaching behind my little brother, I poked him in the back.

Bobby jumped up with a little cry. He sat back down sheepishly. "Th-that was good, Teddy."

"Scared you, didn't I?" I grinned.

"N-no," he said, sitting back down. "I thought I felt a mosquito."

"I was always saying something like that to your father, too," Uncle Curtis said.

"When you told stories?" Bobby asked.

Uncle Curtis nodded. "When our parents thought we were asleep, we used to crawl into one bed and tell stories to one another under the covers."

"Who told the best ones?" I asked.

"Your father," Uncle Curtis said and jabbed his finger at the air. "And he always knew just when to tap me and scare me the most."

"Tell us one of those," Bobby urged.

"Well, since we're talking about snakes, let me tell you about Chinese ones," Uncle Curtis said. "But let me wet my whistle." He poured some water from a canteen into a cup. Then he took a sip.

"Back in China, they take poisonous bugs and reptiles and put them into a jar, and bury the jar at midnight under a full moon. The creatures inside eat one another. And the one that's left becomes magical. This story is about a snake that ate the others.

"Once there was a man who had some business in a faraway town," Uncle Curtis began. "On his way, he met a group of merchants. So he joined them. Now these merchants were a cheerful sort, and they were soon friends. When it was night, they stopped at an inn. But the inn was crowded. And there was only one room left with a big bed. The man was poor, so he stayed in the stables. But his friends stayed in the room."

Uncle Curtis acted out the story pretty good. I was learning a lot about him. Not only could he tell a joke but a scary story as well.

"There were a lot of scary sounds and sights that night. The man barely slept. The next morning, though, the innkeeper told him his friends were gone.

"However, the man was suspicious. He didn't think his new friends would desert him. So he set out on the road, asking people if they had seen his friends. But he was the only traveler that morning. So he went back to the inn. When no one was looking, he snuck into the room where his friends had slept. But there was nothing there but a bed and a chest.

"So the man went to the chest." Uncle Curtis leaned forward and pretended to lift a lid. "And out came the snake."

He told how the man managed to escape. Even so, the ku snake kept coming after him. When the snake had trapped the hero, Uncle Curtis snapped his flashlight on and waved it back and forth. "The magic snake zipped around like a lightning bolt." My eyes followed the flashlight beam as if it were a snake.

"And the snake shot through the air," Uncle Curtis said and lunged with the flashlight at me and Bobby.

And for a moment I was sure I could see a glowing snake. With a scream, my brother and I fell backward off the rock.

"Got you both, boys," Uncle Curtis said, satisfied. He snapped off the flashlight.

"I was just pretending to be scared," I said, getting up. I was sure the seat of my corduroys was covered in mud now.

"S-so was I," Bobby said. "But . . . unh . . . would you please turn on the flashlight again?"

By then the twilight was growing into night.

"Too bad it's cloudy. We'd get some light from the moon and the stars." Uncle Curtis snapped the flashlight back on. "Your turn, Bobby."

Bobby stuck out his legs and gazed at his shoe tips. "I don't know any scary stories."

"Everybody's got to take a turn," I told him.

"I can tell you some stuff that really happened with rattlesnakes," he said, looking up hopefully.

"That'll be fine," Uncle Curtis said.

Bobby licked his lips. "Well, I read this in one of the library books. This guy went camping. And he went hiking. Only he didn't look where he was going. And he stepped on a snake. It was a rattlesnake. The snake got mad and was going to strike. But the guy grabbed a rock and killed it. Then he heard this rattling to his left. And to his right. And all around him. And suddenly he saw all these angry rattlers. So he ran away.

"But that night when he went into his tent, he heard a rattling. And there was a snake on top of his sleeping bag."

The story went on like that. Wherever the guy went, there was always an angry snake wanting revenge.

Suddenly I wished that I hadn't urged him to tell a story. Since we were in rattlesnake country, this was hitting too close to home. All that night, the snakes kept trying to kill the guy in Bobby's story. Each time they got smarter and his escapes got narrower and narrower.

"So he just left everything and ran away. But there was a thick fog, so he couldn't find his car," Bobby said.

Was it my imagination or was there a mist crawling along the ground toward me?

"And all he could hear was this *sss-sss-sss* sound." Bobby made a slithering sound by rubbing his pants leg against a log. "Like a hundred snakes."

When the mist rolled around my legs, my feet seemed to disappear. Suddenly it was so cold that I began to shiver.

"And then he could hear the rattling of a hundred serpents," Bobby said. I don't know when he had done it, but my brother had picked up some pebbles and shook them in his palm. They sounded just like a rattle.

The mist rose higher and higher around me.

"And from out of the fog crawled a rattlesnake.

And it bit him!" When Bobby stamped his foot for emphasis, he broke a twig. There was a loud snap.

I was sure a rattler was leaping at me out of the mist. With a shout, I jumped up.

"Ha, he got you, Teddy." Uncle Curtis laughed, clapping his hands. "Good one, Bobby."

"Thanks," Bobby said, pleased.

"I don't think that was a real story," I said.

"Well, it was in the book," Bobby insisted.

I stared at him. He looked perfectly sincere. I wondered if he was putting me on. Maybe I was underestimating my little brother. I couldn't even out-scare him.

Uncle Curtis stretched and then yawned. "Well, time to turn in, boys. We want to get an early start tomorrow."

Maybe Uncle Curtis was going to sleep tonight. But I didn't think I was.

Suddenly, from within the tent, we heard the sound.

*Sss. Sss. Sssss.*

# ELEVEN 🌲⛺

**Bobby and I were both** too scared to move. Uncle Curtis turned the flashlight on the front of the tent.

But that only drew the attention of the thing. Within the tent, it slithered toward us. I wanted to run, but my legs had suddenly turned to wood.

"St-stay calm, boys," Uncle Curtis said—though he didn't sound very steady himself. He limped forward, stabbing the flashlight beam like a sword. Slowly he shoved the flashlight against the tent flap.

He was a lot braver than me. In Chinatown, Uncle Curtis was a fussbudget. Out here, though, he had his good points. I guess different places bring out different things in people.

The inside of the tent looked as dark as a coal mine. An awful lot of snakes could be hiding in there. Uncle Curtis swung the flashlight slowly in an arc. The next moment he laughed and his shoulders relaxed.

"Well, look who came to visit again," he said. With the flashlight, he spread the tent flap more to the side. In the beam, the raccoon's eyes glowed like yellow marbles.

He was pulling my sleeping bag through the dirt. *Sss. Sss. Sss.*

I was mad, but not mad enough to charge it. "Shoo," I said, waving a hand.

The raccoon looked at us, annoyed. He let go of the bag as if I had spoiled his dinner. Taking his sweet time, he strolled out of the tent. He hadn't bothered to touch Uncle Curtis's shoes or socks.

"You're supposed to be scared of us," I said. "We're bigger than you."

The raccoon simply sniffed at me. He seemed to know we wouldn't hurt him. He just went on, walking away casually.

"I think other campers have been feeding him," Bobby said. "That's why he's so tame."

"Well, he certainly looks well fed," Uncle Curtis said. He scratched his head with the flashlight. "He's huge."

I couldn't help wondering, though, if we had any other visitors inside the tent. Though I listened hard, I couldn't hear anything.

Even so, I suddenly decided that my shoelaces needed to be retied—even if I was going to take them off in just a minute.

From the corner of my eye, I saw Bobby was just as interested in his shoes. So it was Uncle Curtis who went in first.

The raccoon hadn't made as much of a mess as before. Maybe he hadn't had enough time. We straightened up our stuff. Fortunately, the raccoon had only been chomping the bottom corner of my bag. I figured I could stay away from raccoon drool. As I set it up again, I made sure to pat it for snakes. But there weren't any.

"Aren't we going to wash up? We promised Grandmother after all," Bobby reminded us.

"Naw," Uncle Curtis said, "once a day is enough."

Taking off my shoes, I set them by the bag. I'd

use my knapsack as a pillow. Sleeping on the floor, though, hadn't prepared me for this. Our floor didn't have dips and bumps and rocks. No matter how I turned, I couldn't find a comfortable position.

And as soon as I did, I had to go. "Uncle Curtis?" I asked softly. "I need to go to the rest room."

Uncle Curtis stirred in the dark. "Sure. Here's the flashlight. Just follow the path. There are signs," he said with a yawn.

When I peeked out of the tent, it looked awfully dark. I heard all sorts of rustling noises outside. How many ku snakes were out there? And the bushes, which had looked so harmless in the daytime, suddenly bulked as big as monsters.

I told myself I was being silly. And yet I couldn't shake the feeling. If I could have waited for sunrise, I would have. But I couldn't.

I lay there for a little while. Uncle Curtis was already starting to snore. It would serve him right if the ku snake got him first.

I wished now that we had never told scary stories. And I hated what I had become. In

Chinatown, I could handle anything. Up here, though, I was a quivering bowl of Jell-O. I'd been scared to go inside the tent. Now I was too frightened to leave it.

Cautiously I eased out of my sleeping bag. Then I shook out my shoes. So far, no snakes.

Putting on my shoes, I peeked out of the tent. The campground was just as black as I remembered. With the clouds covering the moon and stars, it seemed totally dark.

Snapping on the flashlight, I walked forward slowly. It took a moment to find the sign that pointed to the rest room. Carefully, I followed the path. Finally I saw a tiny light in the distance.

Sure enough I had found the rest room. It was lit by a single dim bulb that shone through the windows, but it was a welcome guide. Now I knew how a ship captain felt when he saw a lighthouse beacon.

I won't tell you about the rest room. Let's just say Grandmother would never go camping. After all, she came to America partly for the indoor plumbing.

I was more confident on the return. But as I

walked along, the flashlight's circle of light got dimmer and dimmer. And then the batteries died completely.

I had never been in a place as dark as this. I didn't realize how much I could miss a street lamp until now. The blackness surrounded me. I felt like I was in the mouth of a giant monster.

I couldn't even see my feet. For all I knew I was trying to walk over a bottomless pit.

And out of the darkness, I heard a *sss-sss*. It's just a raccoon, I told myself. Just a raccoon. But it kept getting closer and closer.

"Shoo, shoo," I said, waving my hand.

*Sss-sss*. In the dark, your mind plays funny tricks. Suddenly I thought it might be the snake man. He had heard me talking about him and had come to get me.

I tried to go on, but stumbled and fell. Sitting up, I desperately clicked the switch of the flashlight.

I gasped when I felt a breeze on the back of my neck. All around the bushes rattled. Was it the magic snake Uncle Curtis had talked about? Had it hidden its light so it could sneak up on me?

I got to my feet and tried to shuffle on. But

something bit my shin. With a shout I went down. It was Bobby's rattlesnake.

I slapped at my ankle. It was only a branch.

*Sss-sss.* The bushes shook near me.

Lifting up the flashlight, I got ready to swing it.

"Teddy?" Bobby called. "Turn on the light."

Relief flooded through me. The hissing hadn't been any sort of snake. It had been Bobby's corduroy pants. "I can't. The batteries died," I said.

"I came looking for you," Bobby said. I heard him close to me, though I couldn't see him.

Great. Rescued by my little brother. Could things get any worse?

"How'd you find me?" I demanded. "It's pitch black."

"Well, it's pretty hard, but I guess I've got eyes like an owl's," Bobby explained. "I should have known you'd be fine."

So fine I was ready to scream in terror. Bobby was made for camping. I was made for a street with lights.

"I thought you'd be hiding in the tent," I laughed nervously. "Those stories were pretty scary, weren't they?"

"Yeah," Bobby agreed. "But then I realized they were imaginary. I was just being pretty silly."

I'd never felt more stupid. He was even braver than me.

"Real silly," I admitted.

"But I'm glad I found you," he confessed. "If I had to go much farther, I think I would have gotten scared again."

Frantically, I tried to think of a way to keep from adding to my shame. Finally I had it. Groping through the darkness, I found his hand. "Here. Feel better?"

He squeezed my fingers. "Yeah."

As we headed back to the tent, I let him take the lead. Just like I was a lost little kid.

"Teddy?" he said.

I tripped over something again but caught myself. "What?"

"You won't tell anyone about my being scared, will you?" he pleaded.

"I wouldn't think of it," I swore. Not when I'd been ready to blubber like a baby.

We stumbled through the darkness. I clutched

his hand desperately so I wouldn't lose him.

I just wish I could have his confidence. Everything was so unfamiliar. Everything was so scary. I started to sweat.

We blundered through bushes and against tents.

The return trip seemed to take even longer than the journey to the rest rooms. Maybe we'd gone too far? Maybe we'd wind up in the bay.

"Gee, I was sure it was over here," Bobby said. I bumped into him when he stopped.

Annoyed, I said, "You said you knew where our camp was."

"I thought I did," Bobby said.

We blundered around for a while. Finally, Bobby said, "We shouldn't have come."

"In the dark, one direction is as good as another," I said.

"No, I mean up here," he said.

I bumped into Bobby again. "I thought you wanted to camp."

I felt my little brother shiver. "It's one thing to read about nature. It's another thing to live in it. And I don't like the cold."

I put my arm around him. "Let's just try to survive the next couple of days. And when we get home, we'll stay there."

I was completely turned around now. "But which way back to the tent?" I was afraid we'd have to wait there all night.

"Wait, what's that?" Bobby asked.

"I don't hear anything, " I confessed.

"Just follow me," Bobby said with new confidence.

"How do you know which way to go?" I demanded. I stumbled after him as I gripped his hand.

"Just listen," he said.

And then I heard the faint buzzing.

"Uncle Curtis!" I said.

His snore was unmistakable. We homed in on the signal like bats.

Once inside the tent, I got the spare batteries from Uncle Curtis's pack. I was grateful for the light when I snapped it on. From the look on Bobby's face, so was he.

I pretended to fluff up my sleeping bag. However, I was really checking for snakes. From the noises next to me, I figured that Bobby was doing the same.

When I had slid inside my bag, I glanced at Bobby. "Ready?"

He was in his already. "Yeah."

When I turned off the flashlight, we were trapped in the blackness again.

I don't think I would have slept much, even if Uncle Curtis hadn't been snoring. The ground was too hard. The air was too cold. And yet it wasn't too chilly for the mosquitoes. Even though they didn't bite me, they buzzed around. Trying to escape them, I burrowed deeper into my bag.

The time just seemed to drag on. Suddenly I heard a yowl like a cat. The next moment Uncle Curtis gave a loud, frightened yell.

Bobby must not have been sleeping either, because right away he snapped on the flashlight. "What is it? What is it?" he demanded.

In the flashlight beam, we saw our neighbor, the raccoon. He was sitting on his hind legs. He had this puzzled look on his face, as if he was wondering what all the fuss was about.

Uncle Curtis was holding his forehead. In

alarm, I thought the raccoon had bitten him. Was the animal rabid?

"Get out, you pest." Grabbing my shoe, I threw it at the intruder.

The raccoon must have been used to that, too. He ducked easily. Then he gave me an indignant stare. Annoyed, he turned around and strolled out of the tent again.

I got out my bag and headed for Uncle Curtis. "Are you okay?"

"I woke up because my forehead suddenly was wet," Uncle Curtis lowered his hand. "But there's no blood," he said, studying his fingers.

I examined his head. "No, it's just moist."

"I think he was licking me," he said. "I felt this little wet, raspy thing. It must have been his tongue."

I retrieved my shoe. "Why? Your face isn't covered in chocolate."

"No," Bobby said thoughtfully, "but animals like salty things, too. Deer look for salty places. They call it a salt lick. Sweat is salty, too, when it dries."

"You mean I should have washed my face?" Uncle Curtis laughed in relief.

"Just like Grandmother said," Bobby agreed.

"Mother knows best after all." Uncle Curtis sighed. "But maybe we shouldn't tell her. She's smug enough already."

"In the meantime, why don't you put some Lion Salve on your head," Bobby said. I heard him taking off the lid.

I took the precaution of smearing some on my forehead too before I passed it on to Uncle Curtis.

You never know.

# TWELVE

**The next morning, I woke up** stiff and cold. I tried to stretch, but I couldn't spread my arms. Then I realized I was inside a sleeping bag. And I was camping. All those aches in my back must be from rocks. I was sure I must look like a waffle.

And then I remembered the night before. Bobby had led me like I was a baby. I'd come up here to prove I was as good as him. What a laugh! No matter what I did, I made a fool out of myself. Everyone was right about me. I belonged in a fish shop. It was Bobby who was the one meant for big things.

For a long time, I just lay, staring up at the tent. I wished I could have been anywhere but here. I hated camping. I only had to put up with this one more day. Then I could leave and never come back. I was a clam who belonged in a fish store.

I closed my eyes, trying to speed up time. Instead, I felt a breeze when the tent flap opened. "Hey," Bobby said, poking me in the side, "Uncle Curtis says we should go soon."

I couldn't look at Bobby. "With his ankles? He's got poison oak."

"He says he can." My brother cleared his throat. "Teddy? Thanks for not ribbing me about last night."

"Forget it," I said. Before I had left home, I would have loved to have done that, but that was before I had humiliated myself so badly.

"You're the neatest brother," he said, squeezing me inside my bag. "Uncle Curtis is taking us for a hike to the ocean."

I guess Uncle Curtis was feeling better. "You mean we're going to *try* to get there," I muttered. "Remember, Uncle Curtis is leading."

"No, he talked to some other campers. They said the trail's really well marked," Bobby said. He held up a folded piece of paper. "And I've got the map. We'll get there for sure."

Bobby saw more adventures. All I saw was more humiliation. "I've seen the ocean. You go. I think I'll stay here."

"What's the matter? Don't you feel well?" Bobby asked.

I rolled over. "I feel sick." Especially of sweet little brothers.

"I'll get Uncle Curtis." Bobby crawled back outside.

The next moment Uncle Curtis limped in. "What's this I hear?" he said. "You're not well?"

"Nope," I said, and added a moan. It always worked on Mother, but not on Uncle Curtis.

"Why don't you get some firewood, Bobby," Uncle Curtis suggested.

"Okay," Bobby said to him and then to me, "I hope you feel better soon, Teddy."

I just gave another groan.

As I heard the tent flap close, Uncle Curtis sat down beside me, careful not to sit on his ankles. "I can tell a fake groan better than anyone else."

"But it really hurts," I said. I winced as I rubbed my stomach.

Uncle Curtis rolled his eyes. "Don't become an actor, Teddy. You don't have the talent. I used to do the same thing when I was your age."

I raised an eyebrow. "You told a fib?" I always figured Uncle Curtis was too stuffy to lie.

"Lots of them," Uncle Curtis chuckled. "Your dad was always the best at sports. And your uncle Mat was always the popular one." He gave me a lopsided smile. "That didn't leave me with much."

"Sometimes," I said cautiously, "I feel that way about Bobby."

Most of Chinatown would have scolded me for picking on my little brother. But not Uncle Curtis. He just tilted back his head. "So that's the way it is. I should have realized."

I tucked my bag up to my chin. "You and Bobby go off and have fun. He's a lot better company anyway."

Uncle Curtis, though, just tapped his fingers on his knee. "I'm sorry, Teddy. This hasn't been much of a birthday present."

That was true, but he sounded so sad. "It's okay," I said. "There's no law that says that gifts have to be perfect."

"But I wanted this one to be." He closed his fingers into a fist. "I really did."

I sat up on one elbow. "Bobby's enjoying it."

Uncle Curtis glanced at me. "But I wanted you to like it."

I decided to take a chance and tell the truth. "Next time take me to a triple feature at the Hub."

"You mean you're giving up already?" Uncle Curtis demanded.

"You're just talking about a stupid hike," I snapped.

Uncle Curtis pursed his lips. "Do you really want to sit in a theater and watch other people do stuff instead?"

"Well," I said, "not when you put it that way."

"If you keep doing the same things over and over, you'll wind up like me," Uncle Curtis said.

It took one clam to know one, I guess. Even so, I tried to lie. "There's nothing wrong with you."

Uncle Curtis laughed softly. "I know what people think of me, but that's okay." He nudged me. "Give the Fun Express one more day. Hike to the ocean with us. You might like it."

I still felt the sting of last night's humiliation. I

wished he'd let me be a clam. All I wanted to do was hide in my sleeping bag, though. "I'd rather rest here."

Uncle Curtis tapped his fingers on the ground. "Well," he said slowly. "Let me put it another way. If you stay, I'll tell Bobby to take care of you."

I sat up out of the sleeping bag. "Hey, that's blackmail!"

"No, it's extortion," he corrected me calmly. "And I'll make sure that Bobby tends to you every minute."

Uncle Curtis really knew how to scare a guy. I let out a groan—a real one this time. I'd been sick one Saturday. Bobby had appointed himself my nurse. He got me water when I wanted it. He got me my comics. But he also talked to me all the time about bugs. It had been more than I could stand. "I guess if I go, he'll be too busy talking to you to bother me."

Uncle Curtis slapped my leg. "You just might see some new stuff, too."

"So far you've lied and threatened," I said, counting off his sins on my fingers.

"You didn't know I had it in me, did you?" He chuckled.

"No," I admitted—not without a little respect.

He got to his knees. "So get up and I'll make toast."

I saw how he winced when he rubbed his ankles the wrong way. "Are you going to be okay?"

He looked more determined than I had ever seen before. "I'll get the Fun Express all the way to the ocean if I have to crawl."

Uncle Curtis had a lot more guts and a lot less sense than I had thought.

I'd gotten dressed by the time Bobby got back with some firewood. He had lots because the wind had blown down branches and twigs. "You're up," he said in surprise.

"Uncle Curtis is a good doctor," I said, glancing at my uncle. He was humming innocently to himself. He knew just what bitter medicine to use.

There was a faucet rearing up from the ground a couple of feet away. I went over to it to wash my face. I was through being a raccoon salt lick. And the smell of Lion Salve was thick in my nose.

"Here, let me help," Bobby said. He snatched my washcloth from my hand and wet it for me.

I stared at Bobby when he held it out. Was he

making fun of me? But all he had was the same sweet smile as always.

Bobby wouldn't be so bad if I didn't have to live with him twenty-four hours a day. If he weren't my brother, I might actually like him.

"Are you still sick?" Bobby asked. "If you are, you just stay here. And I'll take care of you."

I snatched the washcloth from his hand. "I said I was fine."

He leaned forward and peered at my face. "Are you mad at me? You're grumpier than usual."

"I've just got a lot on my mind. That's all." I flapped the washcloth at him. "Thanks, okay?"

"Okay," he said and went bouncing off. That was my little brother. It never took much to make him happy.

The hamburger and hot dogs were still frozen. It was another souvenir of how stupid I was. So we just toasted some buns instead.

I told myself it was all right. Tomorrow I'd be going home. Bobby, of course, was getting more and more excited. Well, let him.

All I wanted to do was not make a fool of myself today.

# **THIRTEEN** ⇡N

**It actually wasn't a bad day** for a hike. The sun had broken through the clouds in spots. Birds were singing. I expected Bambi to wander out at any moment.

A big wooden sign marked the head of the trail. Uncle Curtis waved a hand at it. "You see, boys. This is one trail that's clearly marked. It'll be a piece of cake. All aboard for the Fun Express! Next stop, the beach!"

The path rolled down the slope smooth and easy as it wandered away from camp. It all looked harmless enough. But then all the traps do in the good horror movies.

Uncle Curtis was feeling good after a solid

136

night's sleep. "This way, boys," he declared. Swinging his arms, he waddled forward confidently. "Just tell me if you're having trouble keeping up. Your father and I were like mountain goats when we were your age."

Bobby's canteen bounced against his hip as he trotted after Uncle Curtis. "You used to walk all over?"

"Walk?" he laughed. "That's for sissies. We always ran. We used to race the other kids up the hills," Uncle bragged. "We won every time."

"It's hard to picture Father running anywhere," I said skeptically from the rear. "He's got bunions."

Uncle Curtis glanced over his shoulder. "Believe it or not, Teddy. We were once your age. And your father didn't have bunions back then. We used to call him Speedy."

It was hard to picture either of them being young. "What happened?" I blurted out.

"You'll find out," Uncle Curtis winked knowingly.

"You mean when I grow up?" I asked cautiously.

Uncle Curtis pretended to shoot a pistol at me. "Bingo!"

Bobby, though, didn't have a care in the world. "Hey, there's a Steller's jay," he said, running over to the squawking bird.

"Yeah, it sounds like your uncle Mat." Uncle Curtis laughed. He was still limping, so the poison oak on his ankles must have been bothering him; but he seemed determined not to let it stop him.

I just let the two nature boys babble on. Did I really want to grow old and slow and own a fish store and get bunions? I told myself Uncle Curtis was just joking. And so what if he was telling the truth? As long as I had comics and triple features at the Hub, I'd be fine. At least, that's what I was trying hard to believe.

When Bobby or Uncle Curtis excitedly called my attention to something, I grunted. I was only killing time. There was nothing I wanted to learn. I just didn't want to make a fool of myself.

Anyway, Bobby and Uncle Curtis didn't need me. They were like the squirrels overhead. They just chattered to one another. Every now and then Uncle Curtis tried to draw me into the conversation. But I had already used up my one nature fact. I just nodded instead.

The trees grew over the trail so it was like being in a green tunnel. Little dry leaves littered the path like little potato chips. They crunched under our feet.

I hadn't noticed the air before this. At first it seemed odd. No bus fumes. No city odors. It was different . . . but pleasant. It was sort of cool and dusty. And there was a clean scent that I couldn't place at first. Finally I realized it was all the plants growing around me.

That nature stuff is sneaky. Against my better judgment, I was beginning to enjoy myself. The path didn't seem to be in any hurry to get to the ocean. Neither was I. Jamming my hands into my pockets, I started to lose track of time.

After a while, Bobby started to sing. He was off-key as usual. Uncle Curtis joined in. His voice, though, was flatter than a pancake. And I was feeling so good I joined in.

Grandmother shouldn't have worried about bears. Our singing was enough to scare anything away.

The trail dipped and rose, twisting back on itself like a roller coaster ride. Bobby and I were used to the Chinatown hills, so it was easy.

For a while, a stream ran beside the path. It sounded like water running along the gutter after a downpour. But like the smells, it was nicer. As the stream ran past the rocks, it seemed to chuckle. Every now and then a slight breeze would blow some of the misty air over us.

However, Uncle Curtis's running days had been a long time ago. The engineer of the Fun Express was definitely huffing and puffing like a locomotive as he hobbled along.

"I think . . ." he panted, "Bobby needs . . . a rest."

Bobby glanced at me. I guess he didn't want me teasing him. "I'm fine. Let's keep going."

Uncle Curtis put up a hand. "No, don't . . . push yourself."

I looked at his pale, sweaty face, and I felt sorry for him. It must be awful to get old. I think he was almost thirty-five. "Yeah, don't think you have to show off, Bobby," I said.

"But I—" he started to protest. When he saw me shake my head, he shut up. He knew better than to argue.

Uncle Curtis started toward a tree. "You'll . . . feel . . . better, Bobby. You'll see."

"Uh, Uncle Curtis," I said.

All he could do was nod his head as he shuffled on. "Just . . . a moment, Teddy."

"But you're heading for poison oak again." It was still the only plant I recognized. I pointed to the dark green vine winding its way down from around the tree trunk and spilling over the ground.

Uncle Curtis didn't have enough energy to move on. He just plopped down where he was.

As we sat down next to him by the stream, I saw the little bug with long legs skittering over a calm patch of water. It skated along as easily as if it were ice. "Hey, look at that," I said.

Bobby leaned over beside me. "Neat-o! A water strider!" he declared. Thanks to our neighbor, Charlie, he knew everything about insects.

I didn't care about a funny name. I wanted to know the important stuff. "How does it keep from falling in?" I asked.

"They don't weigh a lot," Bobby explained, "and their weight is shared over those long, long legs. So they don't actually break the surface of the water."

"No kidding," I said.

Poor Uncle Curtis. The Fun Express couldn't even rest now. I just wished he'd put this much energy into taking me to the movies. "They feed on other bugs."

"Really?" I said, impressed.

Uncle Curtis nodded. "Those long legs can pick up the ripples made by its prey. See how short its front legs are? When it skates over to its dinner, it uses those to grab it."

Though I would have died before I let Bobby and Uncle Curtis know, I had to admit some nature stuff could be interesting.

When Uncle Curtis finally struggled to his feet, I was sorry to leave the spot. "Time to start up the Fun Express again, boys."

The trouble started when we came to a fork in the road. The sign with the pointer had fallen over. Uncle Curtis picked it up as if it could tell him the right direction. "Now, that's awkward."

"I got the map," Bobby said. Confidently, he put his hand to his back pocket. Suddenly he frowned. "Hey. It's gone."

"It must have dropped out when we took that break," Uncle Curtis said.

"Well," I said cheerfully, "we'll just have to head back." From there, I might be able to talk them into returning to camp.

Uncle Curtis shook his head. "There's no telling if it's still there." He patted his chest. "But don't worry. Your uncle's the engineer on the Fun Express. He'll get you there. We'll just use the sun."

Bobby scanned the trees, but the tops were too thick, still. "I can't see it. Can you?"

Uncle Curtis set the sign down. He turned slowly in a half-circle and then pointed. "My inner radar says that's west," he said. "If we keep going in that direction, we're bound to hit the ocean."

I'd seen what Uncle Curtis's radar did. If he'd been Columbus's navigator, Columbus would have landed in Italy. "Why don't we look for the map," I said.

"Trust me, Teddy," Uncle Curtis said.

He really thought he had a good sense of direction. I was going to tell him the truth: that he'd be lucky to find the bathroom in his own apartment.

At that moment, Bobby plucked at my sleeve.

"Uncle Curtis is trying so hard to show us a good time. We shouldn't hurt his feelings."

I could see how important this hike was to Uncle Curtis. "Okay, but we're spoiling him," I said.

"Anyway, how lost can you get in a state park?" Bobby grinned.

Those were famous last words, if I ever heard any.

# FOURTEEN

**We had to take** a couple more rests for "Bobby's" sake. Uncle Curtis's hill-racing days were definitely a thing of the past and the poison oak was still bothering him. I didn't even have to prompt my brother to ask for a break. He could see how pale and sweaty our uncle was getting.

If I'd been that out of shape, I would have gone back. Uncle Curtis, though, kept right on plodding along.

After a while, the dense trees gave way to chaparral. The bushes with their shiny green leaves looked like they had just been waxed. They grew like walls on either side. The clouds had covered the sun again, but it had grown warm and muggy.

I felt like I was baking in a green bread pan.

When we came to another fork, we couldn't find a sign. Uncle Curtis scratched his head. "They both look like they're heading sort of west."

"Which way?" Bobby asked.

Uncle Curtis rubbed his chin as he studied both paths. Finally he pointed at the left one. "That's it."

"How can you tell?" I asked.

"I've been there," he snapped.

I couldn't argue with experience, so I didn't say anything each time we hit a signless fork. Uncle Curtis was so confident as he shuffled down his chosen path. By then, we were walking beside pastures. Behind the barbed wire, cattle were grazing or sunning themselves.

My shirt was clammy from all that walking in the humid air. The land rolled on and on like the yellow waves of the sea—with cows surfing on top of them. "How much farther, Uncle Curtis?"

Uncle Curtis wiped his sleeve over his face. "We ought to be seeing the ocean by now."

His rash must have been bothering him because he was limping again. Even so, that didn't slow him down. If Bobby hadn't called for breaks,

Uncle Curtis would have run himself into the ground.

Finally after an hour, one cow looked a lot like another. And even Bobby had stopped pointing at stuff. "When are we going to get to the sea?" I asked our uncle.

Uncle Curtis's cheeks burned bright red. "I think we took a wrong turn somewhere. We better retrace our steps."

"How long has it been since you took this trail?" I asked.

The red spread across his face. "Ten years," he admitted, turning around. I thought we were heading back, but we wound up at a crossroad.

Bobby bent over a flower. "What's this called?"

Uncle Curtis barely glanced at it as he tried to figure out our return route. "I'm afraid that I don't know."

When Bobby was studying something, he could stay for hours. However, I was getting hungry. Unless it was something to eat, I didn't care. Instead, I nudged Uncle Curtis. "I don't remember passing this spot."

Our uncle was looking puzzled himself. It's not

an expression you want to see on your pathfinder and guide. "Gee, we must have gone right when we should have gone left."

So we tried again. Uncle Curtis was going to get us to the sea or die trying. He stumbled along as fast as he could. Only we wound up instead at a field that smelled as if it had just been fertilized.

"Phew," I said, clamping my fingers around my nose. "We were never here. I would have recalled something this stinky."

Uncle Curtis put his hands on his hips in exasperation. "You'd think that there'd be a rancher or ranger to give us some directions."

Bobby massaged his elbow. "Thanks for the tour, Uncle Curtis, but I think we're ready to go to the ocean."

Uncle Curtis turned in a slow circle as if hunting for a sign. When he didn't see any, his shoulders sagged. "I'm afraid that your fearless leader is lost."

Bobby gave him a little worried poke. "Quit trying to put us on, Uncle Curtis."

Uncle Curtis scratched his head sheepishly.

"I'm sorry, Bobby. I really don't know the way out of here."

I pinched my eyebrows together angrily. "But how could you get lost?"

"Apparently with great ease." Uncle Curtis rubbed his ankle in frustration. "The Fun Express has officially run off the track."

Bobby pursed his lips and then he stuck an index finger in the air. "Don't worry. I read something that can help us. All we need to know is the time and then look at our shadow."

Uncle Curtis waved at the ground. "The problem is that we don't have shadows. It's too cloudy."

Sure enough, the clouds had rolled in, hiding the sun completely.

Bobby began to look all around. "Moss always grows on the north side of trees."

"I think it's south." Uncle Curtis frowned.

Anxiously, I started to check the nearby trees. But it's a funny thing: there's never any moss when you need it. "Just our luck. Someone scrubbed the trees."

Bobby screwed up his face and then shrugged.

"I'm sorry. It's my fault. I should have read farther into the manual."

My stomach was growling by now. "We didn't bring any snacks." First things first, after all.

"I wish," Bobby said, "we had dropped bread crumbs behind us."

"Then when the ranger came along to give us a ticket for littering, we could have gotten directions out of here," I said sarcastically. "Good thinking, Bobby."

My brother turned to Uncle Curtis. "What are we going to do?"

Uncle Curtis slapped his sides unhappily. "I guess we keep looking for the trail or find someone to give us directions."

We worked our way back from the flower patch to a little scummy pond. Uncle Curtis kicked a pebble into it. "I don't remember this either. Do you, boys?"

By now, even Bobby was starting to get impatient. "Let's try that way."

We ended up in a little clearing enclosed by huge bushes. And in the center of the circle was an old rusty tub.

"Great," I muttered. We retraced our steps from the tub.

"I don't think we've been in this section at all," Uncle Curtis frowned. "We'd better try to get back to the trees. Once we're there, we can find the right trail again."

Only instead or reaching the woods, we wound up in a weedy meadow where the path ended.

Bobby cupped his hands around his mouth like a megaphone. "Help!" he shouted. "Help!"

I put a hand to his wrists. "Bobby, you're just wasting your breath."

Normally Bobby would have listened to me, but instead he snapped at me. "Well, at least I'm try-ing to do something. I'm not just standing around like a big goof." He looked ready to cry.

"Well, let's take a moment and think anyway," I said.

Bobby, though, stepped away from me and began to yell, "Help, anyone! We're lost!"

Now that we had run across something that wasn't in his books, he was panicking. My little brother was finally feeling as helpless as I was on this camping trip. He was human, after all.

It was the moment I'd been waiting for. I could trumpet it all over Chinatown. But I didn't feel triumphant. Instead, I remembered how he had come to help me last night. As far as little brothers went, I guess I could have done worse.

It's funny how fear is like a germ—it spreads. Uncle Curtis caught it from Bobby. He started to turn in circles. "I was sure I knew the way."

Suddenly I heard a familiar roar. "Hey, it's a car."

I tore through the brush toward the sound. Branches slapped at me. I just hoped there wasn't any poison oak around. Behind me, I could hear Uncle Curtis and Bobby both panting to keep up.

I stumbled out of the bushes on the edge of a two-lane road. Just then, an old pickup truck tore around the bend.

"Hey, hey." Uncle Curtis began to wave his hand.

"Help, help!" Bobby was waving his arms so fast he looked like a windmill.

I added my voice to theirs, too. I never thought I'd want to see that old tent as much as I did now.

The driver took one hand off the wheel to smile

and wave at us from behind the rolled-up window. As he flashed past, I thought I heard loud music from his radio inside.

Bobby started after it. "Wait, wait," he called desperately.

I caught him. "It's no good, Bobby."

He punched at me. "Let me go. He can take us back."

It's odd, but I was calmer than he was. I guess it was because I was used to things going wrong and not having a clue how to solve them.

"You can't catch him," I said. "If we just follow this road, we'll get to help."

"We shouldn't hitch a ride with a stranger anyway," Uncle Curtis said, wiping at his forehead. "What was I thinking?" He dropped his arm.

For once, they listened to me; and we set off after the truck. The nature boys, Uncle Curtis and Bobby, were busy scanning the road for another vehicle.

However, I was strolling along, enjoying the scenery. Now that my feet were on asphalt again, I was feeling comfortable. Dirt and gravel were for Bambi, after all.

So I was the only one who saw the funny branch

sticking up from behind a tree. It shone in the sunlight and had all these straight, shiny twigs.

"That's a funny tree," I said.

"Hey, don't wander off, Teddy," Uncle Curtis said, annoyed.

"But I think I see a television antenna," I said, hurrying along.

I heard them following me as I found a dirt clearing. I might not know a raccoon's tracks from an elephant's. But I knew tire tracks. "It looks like a pick up truck is parked here," I said.

"Hey, there's someone's house," Uncle Curtis crowed. He pointed up a dirt path that led from the clearing.

Actually, it wasn't a house, but a small trailer, an old one with oval sides in green and white metal. I supposed it belonged to a ranch hand or a ranger.

Bobby burst past us to bang at the door. "Hey, hey," he called. "Anyone home?"

Silence.

Bobby slumped. "No one," he said miserably.

Uncle Curtis looked just as disappointed. "That's too bad."

"Now what do we do?" Bobby wondered.

"I guess we could wait here," Uncle Curtis suggested. "Someone's bound to come along."

"Maybe not for days," Bobby said, upset. "We could starve by then. I don't want to see the ocean. I want to go back to camp."

"You and me both, Bobby," Uncle Curtis confessed.

Uncle Curtis looked so tired—like a flounder that had been pounded lifeless. Bobby's lip was quivering. He looked ready to cry his head off.

Bobby might be headed for big things, and I might be stuck in a fish store. But he still needed me sometimes.

"It'll be okay," I tried to assure him.

"How?" Bobby demanded. "We're tired. We're hungry. And we're lost."

That was pretty much it in a nutshell. "What are you so scared about?" I said, trying to calm him. "You weren't frightened last night in the dark."

"I'm not scared of imaginary stuff," Bobby insisted. "But this is real."

Poor Bobby. Maybe it wasn't such a good thing

to be perfect. He never made mistakes, so he didn't know what to do when one came along. But mistakes are my way of life. I was always having to deal with them one way or another.

I guess that was the real difference between us. I could handle an unexpected disaster, and he couldn't. So maybe there was a place for me in the world, too. I might not win the awards and stuff my brother would. But things are always bound to go wrong. And there'll always be a need for someone like me to set them straight.

"So what?" I shrugged. "You know how I'm always screwing up. I always get out of it one way or another."

Uncle Curtis slumped against the trailer. "And how are you going to pull off that miracle?"

"I don't know," I admitted. "But I'll find something." I circled the trailer, noticing several paths that led away. Which one might lead us back to camp?

That's when I happened to look up again at the TV antenna on top of the trailer.

"You know," I said to them, "I bet that's pointing to the TV tower on Mount Sutro." There was a large antenna on a high point in the city from which most of the television stations broadcast their signals.

Bobby frowned. "What kind of camper uses a TV antenna?"

"A lost one," I snapped back and closed my eyes, trying to think. Mount Sutro ought to lie at a very shallow angle to the southwest of Mount Tamalpais. I opened my eyes and studied the antenna. "This way, I think."

"This isn't in any of the camping manuals," Bobby said.

I reminded myself that we were all feeling pretty tired and frustrated. I needed to keep my temper. "Okay. You can stay here and hope the cows learn to talk and give you directions. Or you can come with me."

For the moment, Uncle Curtis and Bobby preferred me to a talking cow. So we trooped down a path. I got a little nervous when we lost sight of the antenna. Fortunately, we came upon a sign. It pointed us to the camp.

"Well," Uncle Curtis admitted, "it's not the way they say to do it in the handbook, but you might as well use anything that works."

"You keep your nature books." I pivoted and blew a kiss in the direction of the trailer. "I'll take TV any day."

As we headed down the trail, Uncle Curtis put a hand on my shoulder. "Good job, Teddy," he grunted.

"You would have thought of it sooner or later."

"Try later," he said. "A lot later—as in never."

It's something to know that you *can* do something that others can't. It made me feel funny inside. Maybe this is how Bobby felt most of the time.

The trail led back through the chaparral in a pretty straight line. I was grateful that we were going back—and that I was the one who had done it.

Uncle Curtis and Bobby had even let me take the point. It didn't matter how tired and hungry I was. I was feeling so good that I started to hum.

Bobby began to sing the same tune, flat as usual. Even Uncle Curtis joined in, off-key.

Since I was the lead, I saw them first. From the corner of my eye, I thought it was two sticks being waved above a rock. When I took a closer look, I saw that the sticks had scales.

I threw out an arm to stop Bobby. "Snakes."

Bobby crowded close eagerly. "What kind?"

Uncle Curtis put his hands on our shoulders. "Stay where you are," he whispered. "They're rattlers."

The rattlesnakes, though, seemed more interested in one another than in us.

"What are they doing?" I asked in a hushed voice.

"I don't know," Bobby said softly.

Uncle Curtis chuckled. "I saw it in a nature show. That, boys, is how rattlesnakes court. Only they usually do it in spring after they wake up from hibernation. I guess this pair doesn't have a calendar."

"Maybe they're mutations," Bobby suggested.

The courtship was like a dance. The two deadly snakes wove in the air like leathery ribbons. Sometimes they curled round and round one another. Sometimes they did circles or twisted their bodies in spirals.

It was funny, but the more I watched, the rattlesnakes actually began to look pretty. Their scales were like beads woven in fancy patterns.

I was still scared of them, and I'd never get close to one. But I wouldn't try to kill them either.

As they slithered away together, Bobby whispered, "Neat-o."

I finally had to admit that maybe there was something more interesting in the world than a triple feature at the Hub, after all—like this nature stuff.

I let out my breath slowly. "Amen."

# ⒻⒾⒻⓉⒺⒺⓃ

**I almost started skipping** when I saw the treetops in the distance. It meant we were getting closer to camp. And it got even better when the path eventually led back to the original trail we had been on.

Through the bushes, I saw the light winking off water. "There's the stream," I said, pointing. I was so hot and tired and dusty that I had never seen a more welcome sight.

"Last one there is an annelid!" Bobby shouted.

He would have started running, but I caught him by the collar. "A what?" I asked suspiciously.

"A worm," he grinned, pulling free.

"In your dreams," I said, plunging after him. However, I remembered poor Uncle Curtis right then. And I glanced over my shoulder. The Fun Express was definitely looking wobbly again. Since he'd been in the rear, neither of us had been watching him. Even though he must have been dying, he hadn't asked for a rest.

"You . . . go on," he puffed. "I'll . . . catch up."

"Naw," I said, jamming my hands into my pockets. "Us clams have got to stick together."

"What?" he gasped.

"I mean, I don't feel like running." I shrugged.

Bobby, of course, had scurried to the bank to look for the water strider. He waved his hand excitedly at us. "Hey, you annelids, there's three striders now."

"Do you mind if I take a break?" I asked Uncle Curtis tactfully.

He mopped his forehead gratefully. "If you want to."

When we got to Bobby, he bubbled, "I wish Charlie was here. She'd love all the insects."

"Or Oscar," I said. His pet alligator would have made a quick snack out of them.

"Have we got something to put them in?" Bobby wondered.

"Forget it, Bobby," Uncle Curtis said as he sank

to the ground. "Your mother gave me one rule: no bringing back new pets."

At home, you couldn't pay me to watch an insect. But water bugs were different. They skated around like they were practicing for the insect Olympics.

"Too bad you can't live your life like that." Uncle Curtis slid his palm through the air. "Just glide along smooth as silk."

I thought of all the disasters on this trip. "No mistakes," I said wistfully.

"Even if you did make a mistake, you wouldn't care," Uncle Curtis said. He reached a hand down to scratch his ankle.

"Like what?" I asked.

"Like making your two favorite nephews go camping," he said.

It was the first time I'd been anyone's favorite anything. "What do you mean?" I asked.

"It's been one blunder after another." Uncle Curtis sighed. "I thought it'd be like the last time when your father and your uncle Mat came with me." He smiled at the memory. "I thought we had a lot of fun."

Since they hadn't had to depend on Uncle Curtis as a navigator, they probably had.

"Then why didn't they want to go on this one?" I asked.

"I guess they didn't have as good a time as I did." He gave his head a sad little shake. "I'm sorry, boys. I told myself I wanted you to enjoy yourselves, but I guess I was being selfish. I really wanted it for me."

I thought of how lonesome he was. "I'm sorry that it didn't work out that way," I said.

"I should have known you can't repeat happy memories." Uncle Curtis rubbed his other ankle. "When Chinatown finds out about this trip, everyone's going to laugh at me. Maybe I'll just drop you boys off and keep on going."

"But it was neat-o," Bobby said. "Or most of it anyway."

I couldn't see why Uncle Curtis was saying it was his fault. There was plenty to share between him and me.

Now, normally I'm glad to weasel out of the blame. However, I thought of how Uncle Curtis had almost crippled himself from poison oak and exhausted himself from walking. He might have set up the camping trip for his own selfish reasons. But then he had tried so hard to make us enjoy it. So I decided to be polite.

"It wasn't so bad." I shrugged. And to my surprise, I found I meant it. Even though I was tired and hungry and dirty, I'd seen the snakes dance.

Uncle Curtis scratched at his legs. "Then . . . you boys aren't mad at me?"

I saw a chance to avoid getting laughed at myself. "Why? As far as anyone knows, we had a great time." I nudged my little brother. "Right, Bobby?"

"Sure," Bobby agreed, "we had a lot of laughs."

"No, Bobby," I coached him. "Nothing funny happened."

Uncle Curtis caught on. "Your parents might not think it was so humorous."

"And then they wouldn't let you go camping again," I cautioned.

Bobby squirmed. "You mean, lie to them?"

"No," Uncle Curtis said slowly. "If they ask you directly, then you tell them the truth."

"But I don't have to answer," Bobby said, nodding slowly as he understood, "if they don't ask."

"That's the ticket." Uncle Curtis winked.

I studied my uncle. I was learning all sorts of new things about him. "You've had practice at that, haven't you?"

Uncle Curtis rolled his eyes. "You know your grandmother. If she had her way, she'd lock all her family up in her apartment. Then she'd be sure we'd be safe."

Maybe I'd been as wrong about Uncle Curtis as I was about nature herself. "But what do we do if they ask us if we got lost?"

"We'll just tell them we got back safe," Bobby suggested.

Maybe there was hope for my little brother after all.

I got out my handkerchief. "It's kind of dirty, but if we soaked it in water, you could put it on an ankle, Uncle Curtis."

Bobby dug out his. His was even grimier than mine. "You can use this on the other."

We soaked them in the stream. Then we tied them around Uncle Curtis's ankles.

"That feels a lot better already," Uncle Curtis said. He started to shove himself up from the ground. "Let's get back to camp."

I grabbed his arm. "What's the rush? This is a nice spot, isn't it?"

Uncle Curtis thought about that and then sat back down. "Yeah, I guess it is."

"It doesn't make sense to rush around just so you can have a good time." I checked a tree behind me. Since it looked clear, I leaned back against it. "Good times will find you if you just wait."

"I didn't think you were a philosopher as well as a pathfinder, Teddy," Uncle Curtis said. He pillowed his head against his hands as he rested on the same trunk.

"I can teach you a lot about relaxing," I promised him.

"I may just take some lessons, Teach," Uncle Curtis said with a wink.

Now that was a promising development. I'd have to see what else I could teach him when we got home.

# SIXTEEN

**If it had been up to Bobby,** he would have stayed the whole day watching water striders. However, after a while, we made him get up and head back to camp.

For a change, things went smoothly, and we got back without any more trouble.

The hamburger and hot dogs were still frozen. But Uncle Curtis found a couple of campers who were leaving. He got the beans and franks and buns at cost.

Naturally, we told scary stories that night. We each used some of the dry ice for effect. The air was still, so the mist puddled on the ground, hiding our feet. And of course, we tried to poke one another at key times to get a scream. We could have told the same stories at home, but it wouldn't have been as much fun.

When I told mine, I pulled out all the stops, adding more and more blood. Uncle Curtis knew some pretty frightening stories about Chinese vampires who would have made Dracula run away. Neither of us, though, could top Bobby. You can't beat nature for gruesome stories.

Both Uncle Curtis and I had to beg Bobby to stop after a while, making him the clear winner.

"Well, I guess we should hit it," Uncle Curtis said.

"But it's our last night here," Bobby wheedled. "Can't we stay up a little longer?"

Uncle Curtis held up his hands. "I don't want to hear any more about what animals eat."

"Then you tell us something," I said.

"You mean another ghost story?" Uncle Curtis asked. "I can't top Bobby."

"Then tell us about when you were a kid in Chinatown," I suggested.

Uncle Curtis scratched his cheeks. "That's ancient history, Teddy."

"Please tell us," Bobby urged.

So Uncle Curtis told us about the old days in Chinatown—when Father was Speedy. He even told us about some of the pranks they used to play. I filed that stuff away carefully inside my head. I was always open to new ideas.

"I didn't know you guys did that sort of stuff," I said with new admiration.

Uncle Curtis started to grin but caught himself. He tried to wag a finger at me sternly. "But don't you do it."

"Of course not," I said, as innocently as I could. At least not much. Behind my back, I had my fingers crossed, so the promise didn't count anyway.

Uncle Curtis, though, guessed the other angle I had in mind. "And don't you blackmail your father either. I told you stuff that not even your mother knows."

"Oh," I said thoughtfully. "So that would be blackmail and not extortion."

Uncle Curtis looked up at heaven for a moment and then sighed. "Somehow, Teddy, you're not learning what you're supposed to on this trip."

"You said camping would be educational," I

assured him, "and it certainly has been."

That night, I was so tired that I even slept okay. The Lion Salve kept both the raccoon and the mosquitoes away. I woke up the next morning just as stiff as the previous day.

However, the clouds had picked up and left, leaving the sky all to the sun. That morning the tent just seemed to fill with light. Bobby and Uncle Curtis were both still snoring, so I slid out of my bag.

The sunset the other day had been pretty enough. But it couldn't hold a candle to this sunrise. I saw the oranges and reds above the treetops. It looked like someone had splashed a paint store over the whole sky. I had to admit you couldn't see a dawn like this in the city. So I just sat on a nearby rock and watched the sun come up.

Breakfast was simple—just toast. And then it was time to break camp. "I'm going to be sorry to go," Bobby said reluctantly.

"I know what you mean," I said.

"Really?" Uncle Curtis seemed pleased. "Then we'll do it again."

"But with regular ice in the chest," I suggested.

Uncle Curtis opened the lid of the ice chest and rapped a knuckle on the hamburger and then on the hot dogs. "I'd leave these for the raccoon, but he'd probably break a tooth."

We rolled up our sleeping bags and brought them with our packs down to the car. I had just gone to get the ice chest when I heard a noise in the tent. I guessed the raccoon was scrounging up one last meal.

"Ha, ha! There's nothing in there," I jeered at him.

The raccoon didn't pay me any more attention than before. He just kept rummaging around inside. And I found myself getting annoyed.

I beat at the side of the tent. "Shoo!" I said.

The raccoon stayed inside, though. He seemed to think I was as harmless as a fly. And that really irritated me. Opening up the tent flap, I kicked my foot inside. "Go on. Get lost."

The raccoon seemed to think I was just doing the cancan for his entertainment. When the noise went on, I started to get angry. "Beat it!" Pulling back my leg, I kicked as hard as I could, thrusting my foot into the tent again.

The tent flap was slightly open so the next instant I caught a whiff of something worse than ten jars of Lion Salve. The odor nearly made me gag. Choking, I fell backward right on my rear end.

The next moment a little black furry head peered out from behind the tent flap. The beady eyes stared at me in annoyance as if to say, "How dare you?"

"Where's the raccoon?" I coughed.

The creature gave a shrug. When he waddled out of the tent, I saw the white stripe running down the black fur on his back.

If I hadn't been so busy gasping, I would have laughed. I should have known Mother Nature would have one last zinger for me. You can talk all you want about the beauties of nature. To me, she'll always be one big whoopee cushion.

I heard footsteps behind me. "Neat-o!" Bobby cried. "A skunk."

"Stay where you are, Bobby," I called. I kept real still myself. One spray of skunk perfume was enough.

The skunk hoisted his tail like a victory flag. Waving it proudly behind him, he marched off into the bushes.

Uncle Curtis was the first one by my side. "Are you okay, Teddy?"

"Yeah, but you're going to have to air out the tent," I said.

Uncle waved a hand in front of his nose. "That's not the only thing we're going to have to clean."

"You stink," Bobby explained simply, and then pinched his nose shut.

Fortunately, the skunk's spray hadn't gotten on my pants. But it was all over my shoe.

I gave Uncle Curtis points. He helped me take it off and then laid it a few yards away. "I think we're going to tie both the tent and this on top of the car."

To my horror, even though the shoe was gone, I still stank. "You'd better add my sock." Unrolling it with my fingers, I flung it after the shoe.

Only the smell still was there. "It must have soaked into your foot, too," Uncle Curtis said, wrinkling his nose.

"That was one potent skunk," I sighed. Would Mother Nature have sent any other kind to see me off?

I tried washing my foot under the faucet; but though I tried and tried, it still reeked.

"I read that tomato juice will get rid of the smell," Bobby said helpfully.

"We'll stop on our way back to Chinatown and clean off your foot and your stuff," Uncle promised. "I know a store that's not too far away from here."

"But what about the tent?" I asked.

"No one will ever have to know," Uncle Curtis promised. "I'll figure out some way to hide the tent until I can air it out."

"Really?" I asked. I'd never expected him to protect my reputation.

"You still want to come back, don't you?" Uncle Curtis asked me cautiously.

Despite skunks and raccoons and trails that weren't there, I decided that camping was worth it. Food never was tastier and stories never scarier. And then there were sunrises like this morning. "Sure," I said.

"Then the three of us are going to protect our little secrets," Uncle Curtis said. "Right, boys?"

"Right," we both promised.

I left the rest of the work to my uncle and brother. With a rag, Uncle Curtis threw away the contaminated shoes and socks. Then I hopped one-footed to the car and got in. Even though we rolled all the windows down, I was already starting to stink up the inside. However, neither Uncle Curtis nor Bobby complained.

However, I minded the smell, so I unrolled the window and managed to stick my foot out the window.

"That's dangerous, Teddy," Bobby said.

"If I don't," I said, "we'll all choke to death before we get off the mountain."

"Don't worry, boys," Uncle Curtis assured us. "I can get to the store by some side roads."

Bobby took Aunt Ethel's map from the glove compartment. "Show me, and I'll be the navigator again."

Uncle Curtis examined the map, turning it several different ways and then handed it back to my brother. "It's not on here."

"Oh," Bobby sighed and dropped the map on the floor.

I just hoped we'd get home by Christmas.

Uncle Curtis called out, "All aboard the Fun Express."

As we rolled away, I twisted around to take one last look behind me. Through the rear window, I saw the bushes stir. And then the raccoon poked his head out of the leaves.

And I was sure he was laughing.

# AFTERWORD

The story is based on several camping trips to Mount Tamalpais and Yosemite that I took with the Boys' Club at St. Mary's Chinese School. Our club was never part of the Boys Clubs of America. It just happened to be a convenient name for our group who met in a room beneath the chapel.

In our group, we numbered some Boy Scouts who, despite pathfinding badges, managed to get us thoroughly lost in the Botanical Gardens in Golden Gate Park one long, long Saturday. However, the most memorable was the attempt to hike from our Mount Tamalpais camp to the ocean. Only a few of us ever made it. I personally never got there. Instead, I was one of those who somehow managed to stumble back to our camp after being lost most of the day. Our poor chaperones were kept busy driving up and down the roads of Marin, picking up the stragglers.

The dry-ice incident really happened, and I'm embarrassed to say that it was my own particular idea. I also once shared a tent with a pair of brothers who insisted on using a Chinese medicinal salve every night.

I've also drawn from family stories about my uncle Francis. It was a bear, not a raccoon, that treated his head like a salt lick, and he was the one who was perfumed by the skunk. His foot smelled so bad that the other campers made him drive with it stuck out the window.

The similarities to the story end there. I would like to emphasize that my uncle Francis was a fine camper, who loved America's national parks. And I want to thank him for his many kindnesses to me.

Furthermore, I want to express my gratitude to all the kind adults who took us camping, as well as my friends who suffered through those cold nights with me. They all tried their best to teach me the delights of the outdoors. It is nobody's fault but my own that my idea of a vacation is still one in which someone else changes the sheets.

I also want to add a word of a warning. At the time, we did not worry about raccoons or their drool on a sleeping bag. However, there are currently some areas of California where raccoons carry a parasite that can cause serious injury to humans. In those areas, raccoons and anything to do with them should be dealt with cautiously.

# LAURENCE YEP

is the author of numerous beloved children's books, including *Cockroach Cooties*, selected for the 2003 Bluebonnet Masterlist; *Later, Gator*; *The Tiger's Apprentice*; *Lady of Ch'iao Kuo: Warrior of the South*; *Dragonwings* and *Dragon's Gate*, both Newbery Honor winners; and an ALA Notable Book, *The Rainbow People*. Mr. Yep was born and raised in San Francisco and currently lives with his wife, author Joanne Ryder, in Pacific Grove, California.